GW01019031

The Ranch War in Riverstoı

Maynooth Studies in Local History

SERIES EDITOR Raymond Gillespie

This year, Maynooth Studies in Local History publishes its 100th study. Over the twenty years of the series these short books have ranged widely, both chronologically and geographically, over the local experience in the Irish past. They have demonstrated the vitality of the study of local history in Ireland and have shown the range of possibilities open to anyone interested in studying local history. From medieval Dalkey to Granard in the 1950s, past volumes in this series have dissected the local experience in the complex and contested social worlds of which it is part. Perhaps inevitably, many have concentrated on well-established paths of enquiry with works on the Famine of the 1840s and the late 19th-century land war, while others reveal the riches that await gathering from the medieval and early modern worlds. The sister series, Maynooth Research Guides in Local History, has also facilitated access to these worlds by providing reliable and user-friendly resources that help those unfamiliar with the raw evidence to deal with the sometimes difficult sources that survive from the more remote past. Studies of local worlds over such long periods are vital for the future since they not only stretch the historical imagination but provide a longer perspective on the evolution of local societies in Ireland and help us to understand more fully the complex evolution of the Irish experience. The existence of a large body of published studies, which are not a simple chronicling of events relating to an area within administrative or geographically determined boundaries, opens the possibility of comparative study to allow us to see better why particular regions had their own personality in the past. Such an exercise is clearly one of the most exciting challenges for the future.

Like previous volumes in the series, the six short books published as part of this centenary offering are reconstructions of the socially diverse worlds of the poor as well as the rich, women as well as men, and reconstruct the way in which those who inhabited those worlds lived their daily lives, often little affected by the large themes that dominate the writing of national history. In addressing these issues, studies such as those presented in these short books, are at the forefront of Irish historical research and represent some of the most innovative and exciting work being undertaken in Irish history today. They also provide models that others can follow up and adapt in their own studies of the Irish past. In such ways will we understand better the regional diversity of Ireland and the social and cultural basis for that diversity. These books convey the vibrancy and excitement of the world of Irish local history today

Maynooth Studies in Local History: Number 105

The Ranch War in Riverstown, Co. Sligo, 1908: 'A reign of terror, intimidation and boycotting'

Patrick Cosgrove

FOUR COURTS PRESS

Set in 10pt on 12pt Bembo by
Carrigboy Typesetting Services for
FOUR COURTS PRESS LTD
7 Malpas Street, Dublin 8, Ireland
www.fourcourtspress.ie
and in North America for
FOUR COURTS PRESS
c/o ISBS, 920 N.E. 58th Avenue, Suite 300, Portland, OR 97213.

ISBN 978-1-84682-357-2

Printed in England by
Antony Rowe Ltd, Chippenham, Wilts.

FIGURES

Acknowledgments

Sincere thanks are due to Pr
contribution to this ser
thanks are also due to
guidance and insight
comments on ear
grateful to th
Maynoot
Natior
Sli

...fessor Raymond Gillespie for accepting my ... and for his patience and encouragement. My ... Dr Terence Dooley for being a constant source of ... Both he and Dr Karol Mullaney-Dignam provided useful ... drafts of this work and for that I am grateful. I am also ... staff of the John Paul II library and Russell library at NUI ... National Library of Ireland, National Archives of Ireland, The ... Archives (UK), Kew, the Public Record Office of Northern Ireland, ... Folk Park and Sligo County Library, as well as friends and colleagues. Finally, a very special thanks to my family and to Karol, for their continued support.

Introduction

The Irish Land Act of 1903, better known as the Wyndham Act (after George Wyndham, then Conservative chief secretary of Ireland), resulted in the sale of a huge number of estates across Ireland. While landlords were encouraged to sell by virtue of a 12 per cent cash bonus in addition to the purchase money, the act also ensured that the tenant-purchasers' annuities would be appreciably less than their former rents. Although this proved to be a major incentive for tenants to purchase, many small farmers with uneconomic holdings found that even after purchase they required more land to make their farms economically viable. The Wyndham Act contained provisions whereby any untenanted land sold along with an estate could be divided up among uneconomic small holders, their sons and others in the locality. This raised expectations in rural Ireland among small farmers, agricultural labourers, evicted tenants and the landless who all hoped to obtain a parcel of land. This land hunger was also experienced by those who were not uneconomic small holders but who were anxious to benefit from the possible redistribution of untenanted grazing lands in their locality. This brought into being a period of 'anti-grazing' agitation between 1906 and 1909, known as the Ranch War, which spread across much of Connacht, the midlands and north Munster. In 1908, the Liberal chief secretary of Ireland, Augustine Birrell, identified the prevalent mood in many parts of rural Ireland during these years:

> Many people who were in no sense of the word congested tenants have shared in the division of untenanted land. Hopes have been excited; land hungry eyes have been greedily cast on the untenanted land by persons living in the district; they marked them for their own. Parochialism has prevailed over nationalism in this matter.[1]

The large-scale stock-rearing grazing ranches, which often formed part of landlords' estates, became the obvious source of additional land. Many landlords, although they might have sold the tenanted parts of their estate, were keen to hold on to such grazing lands, which they rented out on the profitable eleven-months system. This involved the letting of untenanted land on eleven-month leases, thereby avoiding the rent-fixing system of the land courts which dealt with permanent tenancies of twelve months or more. The obvious attraction of the eleven months system for landlords was that rents were set by market demand rather than being subject to the land courts. The Ranch War largely grew out of a demand to have these grazing ranches divided up or redistributed among those in their locality. In order to force landlords to relinquish such untenanted land, agitators targeted graziers and others who rented the land, thereby removing the market demand and bringing pressure to bear on landlords to sell to the Land Commission. Although the leadership of the Irish Parliamentary Party (IPP) was initially slow to support such agitation, many party members, including Laurence Ginnell, the MP for North Westmeath and David Sheehy, the MP for South Meath, actively promoted it. On the advice of Ginnell, the first known case of 'cattle-driving' in the Ranch War occurred at Tonlagee, Co. Roscommon, in October 1906, when cattle belonging to John Beirne were removed from his grazing farm and scattered throughout the locality. Soon after, Beirne surrendered the farm for redistribution.[2] The agitation quickly spread and at its height took in the counties of Roscommon, Galway, Leitrim, Mayo, Tipperary, King's County (Offaly), Queen's County (Laois), Meath, Westmeath, Clare, Longford and Sligo, the focus of this study.

The county of Sligo had two members of parliament: P.A. McHugh (1859–1909), who represented North Sligo and John O'Dowd (1856–1937), who represented South Sligo. Both men were members of the IPP, led by John Redmond, whose ultimate goal was to secure home rule. McHugh was a journalist and the owner and editor of the *Sligo Champion* newspaper. A native of Co. Leitrim, he came from a radical agrarian background having been imprisoned during the Plan of Campaign, 1886–91.[3] He played an important role in the establishment of the United Irish League (UIL), which was formed in 1898 by a Cork native, William O'Brien, with the aim of getting the grazing ranches divided.[4] While he was sympathetic towards the anti-grazing agitation known as the Ranch War, ill-health restricted his activities prior to his death in 1909. His colleague O'Dowd, a native of Bunninadden, Co. Sligo, was a farmer and a merchant who had spent time in America as a young man. He was a former Fenian who had been involved in the Irish National Land League and was imprisoned during the Land War of the 1880s.[5]

Both McHugh and O'Dowd dominated nationalist politics in their respective constituencies and were heavily involved in the UIL, the most prominent and active organization in the county. After all, John Redmond, the leader of the IPP, was also the president of the national directory of the UIL. Thus, in Co. Sligo, the UIL was organized along similar lines to the two parliamentary constituencies: North Sligo and South Sligo. Local UIL branches had representation on the North Sligo or South Sligo UIL executive committees, both of which were headed by the local MP. Most of the agitation in Co. Sligo during the Ranch War occurred in the south of the county with its epicentre at Riverstown which had a strong and aggressive UIL branch there. There were many other active branches in the region including those

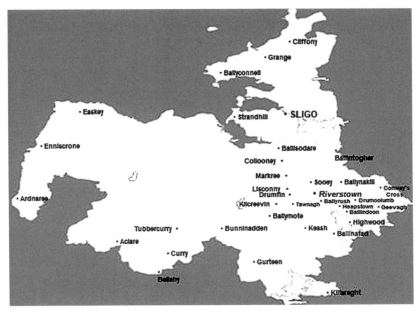

1 Map of Co. Sligo

at Ballyrush, Kilcreevan, Highwood, Sooey, Conway's Cross, Geevagh, Killaraght, Bunninadden, Moylough and Ballymote. Notable members of the South Sligo UIL executive included John Gilmartin, the vice-chairman of the Sligo Board of Guardians and C.W.P. Cogan, a prominent UIL organizer and agitator.[6]

Geographically almost half-way between Boyle, Co. Roscommon and Sligo town, Riverstown is located in the south-east of Co. Sligo, north of Lough Arrow and east of Ballymote. The village is situated on low-lying land between the rivers Unchin and Douglas and was not only divided between two parishes, Kilmacallan and Drumcolumb, but also between two estates. The O'Hara's Coopershill estate was on the Drumfin side of the Unchin river while on the other side lay the estate of the Coopers of Markree.[7] In terms of policing by the Royal Irish Constabulary (RIC), Co. Sligo comprised five RIC districts: Easkey, Collooney, Sligo, Tubbercurry and Ballymote, the latter covering the Riverstown area. According to the census of 1901, the population of Co. Sligo stood at 84,083 with 90.56 per cent being returned as Roman Catholic. The majority of the non-Catholic population were located in the North Sligo parliamentary division although there were sizeable communities in many areas in the South Sligo parliamentary division including the Riverstown District Electoral Division (DED). This DED included portions of the parishes of Kilmacallan, Drumcolumb and Tawnagh, all in the barony of Tirerrill and had a population of 879. Of that total, there were 677 Roman

Catholics, 159 Protestant Episcopalians, nine Presbyterians and 34 Methodists. The Protestant Episcopalian and Presbyterian elements of the population were primarily located in the parishes of Drumcolumb and Kilmacallan while the Methodist community was most numerous in Tawnagh parish.[8]

The pace of land purchase in Co. Sligo under the Wyndham Land Act of 1903 had been steady but unspectacular. Landlords such as Sir Jocelyn Gore-Booth of Lissadell, Charles Phibbs of Doobeg, Major Robert W. Hillas of Doonecoy (Seaview), Owen Wynne of Hazelwood, Colonel John Howley of Portsmouth, England and Utred A. Knox of Ballina, Co. Mayo, took advantage of the favourable provisions of the act to sell off portions of their estates. According to a 1909 report of the Estates Commissioners, the body within the Land Commission who administered the 1903 Land Act, 2,636 tenants had purchased land to the value of £589,532 on 52 estates in the county by 31 March 1909 – although there were further sales which had not yet been fully processed by this date. Nevertheless, this still left Sligo behind the counties of Galway, Roscommon and Mayo, both in terms of the number of tenant-purchasers created and the volume of land that had changed hands.[9]

The redistribution of untenanted land had also been languorous. In 1906, a parliamentary return of untenanted land in Irish rural districts revealed that there were 191 acres of untenanted land in the Riverstown electoral division. Neighbouring electoral divisions such as Drumcolumb, Lisconny, Drumfin, Lakeview and Ballynakill contained 386, 1,125, 734, 132 and 526 acres of untenanted land respectively.[10] Surrounding these swathes of untenanted land were numerous small holdings. In the Riverstown electoral division alone, 176 out of 193 holdings were found to be below 50 acres in size with 101 of these being less than 15 acres.[11] There was an obvious demand for the compulsory purchase and redistribution of all the untenanted land in the south Sligo region as revealed in evidence given by Patrick Dyar, a member of the UIL from Tubbercurry, before the Royal Commission on Congestion in April 1907, when he stated:

> By drawing a line from Bunninadden to Collooney, thence to Riverstown, Ballyrush, Keash, and Bunninadden you get a rough boundary of a fertile district from which the tenants were practically wiped out during the clearances of the forties and fifties. Large tracts of land sufficient to provide economic holdings for between five hundred and six hundred families, besides enlarging the holdings of the present small occupiers and still leaving ample grazing lands, are untenanted or not occupied by resident tenants or landlords in this area.[12]

By referring to clearances which occurred during the Great Famine of 1845–51, Dyar subtly emphasized the historic claim of the victims' descendants to the 'abundant' tracts of untenanted land in these localities.

Drawing on a wide range of primary source evidence, including police reports, newspaper accounts, parliamentary papers and Hansard parliamentary debates, this study examines the Ranch War as it developed in south Sligo in 1908 and 1909. Any research on this period owes much to David Seth Jones' in-depth study of the grazier class, Miriam Moffitt's work on the social and political experiences of Connacht's Protestant community, as well as the work of Paul Bew, Philip Bull and Fergus Campbell, who have all dealt with the Ranch War in their studies on land and nationalist politics in the late 19th and early 20th centuries.[13] In addition to addressing these themes, this local study offers interesting perspectives on other issues concerning early 20th-century rural Ireland, including the importation of firearms and the difficulties faced by the state authorities in maintaining law and order amid unrelenting demands for the break-up of grazing ranches, and the role of local newspapers as agents of agitation to this end. Local studies, such as John McTernan's *Olde Sligoe: aspects of town and county over 750 years* (1996) and Jack Johnston (ed.), *The Riverstown story, County Sligo* (2005), provided useful starting points for investigating the effects of the Ranch War on local communities in the county. In this context, the first chapter of this study considers the manifestations of 'anti-grazing' agitation at a local level in the south of the county and deals in detail with the various activities of local UIL branches. The second chapter focuses on the fallout from one of the most dramatic and sensational incidents of the agitation: the shooting of a young man named John Stenson at a cattle-drive in Riverstown in October 1908. At this time, the Riverstown UIL branch was operating a boycott of local Protestants (who refused to join or subscribe to the league), which led to a government prosecution known as the 'Riverstown conspiracy' case. The third chapter looks at the revelations which emerged during the case hearings about the operation of this boycott and about the plight of the loyal Protestant minority. While the various incidents at Riverstown may have been parochial in nature, they quickly acquired national significance and, as this study reveals, attracted the attention of the leading politicians of the day.

1. 'The law of the league'

Before examining the Ranch War in south Co. Sligo, it is important to understand the sense of expectation that existed by 1908, not only in that county but elsewhere in rural Ireland, regarding the introduction of a new land act. Early in that year, the Liberal chief secretary, Augustine Birrell, promised to introduce legislation to amend the Wyndham Land Act of 1903, raising hopes that the Land Commission would be given powers to compulsorily acquire and redistribute untenanted land. This sense of anticipation was heightened by the release of the report of a Royal Commission on Congestion in May 1908. According to Birrell, 'the excitement and interest occasioned by that commission all over Ireland could not be exaggerated. What had happened? The commission had reported in favour of this very thing, namely, the handing over of the grasslands.'[1] In what appears to have been an attempt to defuse anti-grazing agitation, the chief secretary prematurely introduced his land bill in late November 1908. Being late in the parliamentary session, there was little time for debate and while the bill would be reintroduced at the beginning of the 1909 parliamentary session it would be December 1909 before it was passed into law.

In the interim, matters were taken in hand at a local level by the UIL who were so effective that, as early as March 1908, Justice George Wright remarked that 'the only law feared and obeyed is the law, not of the land, but of the United Irish League'.[2] By increasing the intensity and extent of agitation, the league sustained pressure on the government to introduce legislation that would satisfactorily address the demand for greater acquisition and redistribution of untenanted land. Riverstown UIL and the surrounding branches relied on a number of tactics to achieve this objective and particularly to put pressure on those who might have taken an evicted farm or grazing land on the eleven months system. Individuals perceived as having violated the 'law of the league' by these or other means were typically branded as 'objectionable' by the UIL and became victims of some form of agitation. The most notable feature of the Ranch War agitation was cattle-driving, which could occur during the day or at night and usually involved removing cattle, or other stock, from their field and scattering them in all directions. Depending on the force used, the animals frequently returned lame or with serious injuries resulting from being forced over ditches and walls or being continuously driven for many miles down country roads. Thus, the owner usually suffered a pecuniary loss as injuries to the animals depreciated their value while walls demolished and gates broken, to ensure the animals' escape, required repairs. Much of the cattle-driving around the Riverstown district appears to have taken place at night, presumably to avail of the cover of darkness and to avoid identification by the police. Cattle-driving had an important social and communal aspect with large crowds participating although it could just as easily be accomplished by a few well-organized men.

This sense of social and communal participation was also reinforced by regular band parades which created a sense of ceremony, drama and spectacle. Most UIL branches in the south Sligo region were closely linked or affiliated with a local band, which was regularly used as an instrument of intimidation. The bands would parade, usually in the evenings, around the grazing ranches or the homes of those considered 'objectionable' or in the general vicinity if confronted by the police. The bands featured a number of different musical instruments such as fifes and horns but virtually all contained a drum, which led to those involved often being referred to as 'drumming parties'. As it was well known that the object was to intimidate, the bands rarely committed any 'overt act' that could result in a prosecution. Consequently, the Inspector of the RIC in Co. Sligo, James E. Holmes, acknowledged that the 'police have a very difficult task in dealing with the band parades'.[3] A band did not have to stop and play outside an individual's house to 'mark him "objectionable"'. Sometimes, they simply stopped playing at the house and passed in silence, which proved equally effective in signalling the object of their intent. Bands regularly attended and played at public meetings, demonstrations and rallies attended by large crowds and addressed by the local MP or other leading nationalists in the area. In some instances, such gatherings were held at grazing farms which the UIL wished to have divided – or somewhere in the vicinity when police intervened – the objective being to pressurize the holders of the farms to relinquish them. The secretary of the South Sligo executive of the UIL, John Gilmartin and the UIL organizer, C.W.P. Cogan, regularly spoke at these events and were renowned for their inflammatory rhetoric. These men often publicly named 'objectionable' individuals and advised their audience on how to treat them.

Boycotting was another favoured tactic used by the UIL against 'objectionables' and was essentially a form of social ostracization. Boycotted persons were shunned by the other members of the community, shops refused to serve them, labourers refused to work for them and so forth. They might be forced to travel many miles to another town to obtain supplies and often found that no one would buy their cattle or produce when they attempted to sell it. The severity of the boycotting varied depending on the organization and determination of those who sought to enforce it. Intimidation regularly extended beyond the 'objectionable' person with the individual's family being shouted, 'groaned' or 'hooted' at when they went out in public. The Ballyrush

UIL branch, for example, attempted in conjunction with the local band to boycott a local landlord, Captain McTernan, in order to force him to give up a piece of his demesne to a member of the branch – even though the police believed that the man had 'no earthly claim to it'. On the night of 12 March 1908, the Ballyrush band were followed by a crowd as they paraded back and forth before Captain McTernan's residence at Heapstown and by the house of one of his workmen, despite the presence of the police. Following an altercation, nine men were arrested and brought before the resident magistrate with seven entering into sureties for good behaviour and two going to jail for a month in default.[4] Resident magistrates featured prominently in the local justice system and were directly answerable to the chief secretary of Ireland. They were required to be resident in the district for which they had responsibility and administered the petty sessions courts as well as the majority of the magisterial duties in that district.[5]

A significant agent of UIL agitation was the local press, which diligently reported the speeches given at demonstrations as well as the minutes of the local branch meetings. Newspapers like the *Roscommon Herald* and particularly the *Sligo Champion* regularly published intimidatory resolutions passed at UIL meetings which condemned individuals by name. As the County Inspector of the RIC outlined: 'All their boycotting & intimidatory resolutions & decisions are published in the *Sligo Champion*, which gives them increased power.'[6] By publishing such material, the newspaper facilitated the intimidation of those who had come to the attention of local UIL branches for various reasons. The UIL 'courts' were another feature of many branches and their decisions, concerning all matters connected with land and other issues in their localities, also regularly appeared in the *Sligo Champion*. Even the police acknowledged that the 'influence of the UIL' was so widespread that 'its branch tribunals adjudicate upon everything'.[7] Indeed, so great was the 'dread of the league' that the majority of people who were called to appear before these 'tribunals' automatically submitted to their decisions.[8] A Mr Frazer who rented some grazing land near Highwood proved the exception rather than the rule when he went to the police with a letter he had received from the local UIL branch secretary calling on him to come before the branch and explain his conduct.[9] While it seems that Frazer did not come to any physical harm, others were not so lucky. A herdsman working on a grazing farm in Bunninadden, for instance, who had presumably already been warned to cease work at the farm, was attacked and beaten by members of the local branch when encountered in a public house in Ballymote.[10]

With a new land bill eagerly anticipated and the report of the Royal Commission on Congestion advocating the purchase and redistribution of untenanted land by the Land Commission, the UIL branches at Riverstown and elsewhere in south Sligo showed increased signs of activity from the late spring of 1908. The South Sligo executive of the UIL set the tone at a meeting on 8 April 1908 in Ballymote where it was decided that the police should no longer be supplied with rented cars for transport. A few days after the resolution, a man who drove the Head Constable of Ballymote was called before that branch to explain his conduct. Consequently, he later refused a car to the Head Constable admitting he was afraid to carry him. Despite offering to pay three times the regular fare the County Inspector of the RIC stated, in his report for April 1908, that the police were now unable to obtain any cars in Ballymote.[11] The South Sligo UIL executive had also passed a resolution at the Ballymote meeting condemning the eleven months system and called on all nationalists to refrain from sending cattle to the grazing ranches. Those who violated the resolution were to be 'classed as enemies to the nationalist cause'.[12] Such individuals could be branded an 'objectionable' and faced the prospect of cattle-drives, boycotting, band parades and various other forms of intimidation. This increased activity by the UIL in south Sligo did not pass without comment. Speaking as a member of the Irish Unionist Alliance, Captain Bryan Cooper of Markree Castle, Collooney, outlined to an English audience at Colchester how the 'tyranny of the United Irish League' dominated many western districts including the area around his family estate.[13]

In order to 'concentrate public attention on the grazing system and inaugurate a determined campaign against its continuance in the district', a large UIL demonstration was held in Riverstown on 26 April 1908 and was attended by contingents from south Sligo, north Roscommon and north Leitrim. Thomas Culhane, a member of the local UIL branch, a shopkeeper and farmer, set the tone by telling the audience that 'grazing would no longer be tolerated within Riverstown and its confines'. The MP for South Sligo and chairman of the South Sligo UIL executive, John O'Dowd, called for the grass ranches to be split up and advised the people to rely on the old methods of agitation which had proved successful in the Land War of the 1880s. These denunciations of the grazing system and O'Dowd's advocacy of cattle-driving quickly manifested itself in a series of drives.[14] Over the following weeks over 400 animals belonging to Robert Gorman of Sligo were 'driven' at Riverstown and all the stock on Captain McTernan's farm at Heapstown was scattered. The *Sligo Champion* reported how the Riverstown and Ballyrush bands paraded nightly around the grazing farms in the district, followed by the police, and that 'cattle, sheep, and horses, too numerous to count, are to be seen wandering along the roads miles away from the farms'.[15]

The presence in the area of the paid UIL organizer, C.W.P. Cogan, who had been involved in agitation elsewhere in Connacht and in Co. Longford, undoubtedly contributed to the increased activity of the UIL branches in south Sligo. After he addressed a late-night meeting, in May 1908, chaired by Thomas O'Gara of the Riverstown UIL branch at Tawnagh crossroads, where a

torchlight procession and a huge bonfire added to the theatre and spectacle of
the event, a number of cattle-drives occurred in the district later that night.
In order to try to address these disturbances in the Riverstown district, police
from other stations elsewhere in Co. Sligo were sent to the area and by May
1908, the RIC County Inspector acknowledged that it would be necessary to
request additional manpower from outside of the county.[16]

Central to the increased activity in the Riverstown district was the
reorganization of the Riverstown UIL branch in May 1908 (see Appendix A).
The new branch president, Thomas J. Judge, was the son of John Henry Judge,
a publican and general merchant in the town. The police suspected that
Thomas J. Judge might have been involved in the so-called Jameson raid in
1895 and possibly fought against the Boers in the Boer War (1899–1902) in
South Africa, before his return home to Riverstown.[17] The RIC County
Inspector, James E. Holmes, considered him 'a very bad lot' and 'at the bottom
of all the mischief at Riverstown.' The police believed that his father had
turned him out not long after his return from South Africa but soon took him
back in again – on the advice of the Catholic parish priest, Canon Meagher,
who now apparently regretted his intervention.[18] Any differences with his
father were evidently resolved as he took over the running of premises in
Ballintogher, not far from Riverstown, where his father was attempting to
expand his business. In the 1901 census Thomas can be found in Ballintogher
where he held a 'public house' and listed his occupation as a 'shopkeeper'.
However, by 1908 he appears to have returned to Riverstown and was involved
in the family business in the village.[19]

The other key members of the newly reorganized UIL branch were:
Thomas O'Gara, a builder and a district councillor who was elected vice-
president, John McDermott, the son of Bernard McDermott, a blacksmith,
who was elected deputy vice-president and Thomas Cawley, a 'farm servant'
with relatives at Emlagh, who became secretary of the branch.[20] The censuses
of Ireland for 1901 and 1911 provide details of the social, economic, religious
and marital circumstances of these men, who held positions of power within
the branch, and the men who sat on its committee. Branch committee
members were appointed to represent different townlands in the locality of
Riverstown and the majority of these listed their occupation as 'farmer's son'
or 'farmer'. In many cases, their father was still alive and probably still in control
of the family farm, which indicates that, although they may have expected to
inherit, a significant proportion did not actually hold farms. Others were
agricultural labourers or tradesmen from agricultural backgrounds. Hardly any
of the men were younger than 30 years of age in 1908 and approximately half
of them were unmarried. The attendees at the reorganization meeting in May
1908 were described by the *Sligo Champion* as 'nationalists of the district,
including labourers, artisans, town tenants, and farmers'.[21] However, the County

2 The leadership of Riverstown UIL branch (clockwise, left to right):
Thomas J. Judge, John McDermott, Thomas Cawley, Thomas O'Gara.
Source: *Roscommon Herald*, 7, 14 Nov. 1908 and 13 Mar. 1909.

Inspector of the RIC viewed these men, whom he regarded as the principal
agrarian agitators in the Riverstown area, as 'a set of idle fellows who hold no
law whatever – carpenters, tailors, cattle jobbers, sons of a publican & a
blacksmith.'[22]
    The activities of the Riverstown and surrounding UIL branches can best
be gauged by examining the case of the Knockalassa farm just outside
Riverstown. Matthew McDermott, of Annagh, Ballindoon, had recently
purchased the farm from the Land Commission to whom he was paying
purchase annuities. Prior to purchase, the farm, which consisted of 69 Irish
acres, had been let on the eleven months system and there were those in the
locality who felt that the farm should have been divided among the small
farmers and labourers in the locality. McDermott was declared a 'grabber' and
he and his family were boycotted. They were refused supplies in Riverstown
and had to travel to Sligo town for their goods. The family were subjected to
various forms of intimidation such as 'booing and shouting' whenever they
ventured out and resolutions appeared in the local press condemning Matthew
McDermott. Even those who associated with the 'Knockalassa grabber', as he
soon became known, were swiftly taken to task by Riverstown UIL; a man

named Michael Hannan was brought before a meeting of the local branch and promised in future to have 'no connection whatsoever' with him. At the same meeting, Dick Brennan, Michael Higgins and Mark Colgan were also condemned for their continued association with McDermott.[23] The effectiveness of such resolutions, especially where individuals were publicly named, was significantly increased by their publication in the *Sligo Champion*. Thus, not only were people in the region made aware of who was being boycotted but they also quickly became conscious of the consequences of being associated with boycotted people like the McDermotts. The possibility arose that by failing to comply with the league's directives they too could be subjected to boycotting or other forms of intimidation. On a Sunday morning, 24 May 1908, the same day that the Riverstown UIL branch was reorganized, a group of men on bicycles, reportedly disguised as women, drove the cattle off the Knockalassa farm and scattered them throughout the locality. Upon returning from Mass, Patrick McDermott, Matthew's son, who lived on the farm, found that parts of a stone wall had been knocked down and that all the animals had disappeared. The police later located the animals over six miles away in Ballymote and many were injured or lame from being 'driven'. The county court judge, John Wakely, would later award Matthew McDermott over £21 compensation for malicious injuries to his animals which was levied on the townlands of Ardkeeran, Tawnagh and Heapstown, all in the vicinity of Riverstown and deemed responsible for 'doing the boycotting'.[24]

The occurrence of cattle-drives during the day-time, such as that at Knockalassa, tended to be the exception rather than the rule in Co. Sligo where the majority occurred at night. One infamous night drive occurred on the McClintock grazing farm at Coolbock, Riverstown, in early May 1908 when over 100 animals were scattered throughout the area, with placards suspended from their necks bearing the words 'Ireland for the Irish and the land for the people'.[25] Given the increase in cattle-driving and other forms of agitation, it was no surprise that, on 12 June 1908, Sligo joined Galway, Clare, King's County, Leitrim, Roscommon and Longford on a list of counties proclaimed, under legislation introduced in the reign of William IV (An act to consolidate the laws relating to the constabulary force in Ireland, 1836), to be in a state of disturbance and necessitating extra police cover.[26] In Co. Sligo 206 policemen were already serving and despite the addition, in June 1908, of an additional 30, the majority of whom were posted to the Riverstown district, the County Inspector of the RIC acknowledged that the 'Riverstown leaguers' had 'lost all regard for law'. According to him, conditions were steadily deteriorating in the area: 'The disturbance is organized by the UIL & takes the form of intimidation by cattle-driving, & of band demonstrations in the vicinity of lands & homes occupied by persons who are termed by the league as "objectionables". The bands are followed by large crowds night after night.'[27]

Further cattle-drives took place in the Riverstown district between 21 and 23 June 1908. The Cams farm, located between Riverstown and Ballymote, and two farms held at Tawnagh on the eleven months system (one by the Dukes of Newpark at Newtown and the other by a Dr Duke, who resided in London) were cleared of all stock. Emboldened by success, the cattle-drivers succeeded in clearing the lands of Owen Phibbs, DL, of Seafield (Lisheen) at Ardcumber, beside Riverstown village, late on the night of 26 June despite the presence of the police.[28] Over 100 men participated in the drive and when a police patrol endeavoured to get close enough to identify some of the men they were 'called foul names & pelted with stones'.[29] Later that same night, at around 2.30 a.m., the Riverstown band, upon returning from parading near the grazing farms in the district, attempted to scatter the very cattle that the police were returning to the Ardcumber farm. Nine men would later be arrested to appear at Riverstown court on charges of unlawful assembly. RIC Sergeant John Reilly explained, in his evidence, how the band had visited 'all the grazing farms in the vicinity with the object of intimidating the owners and persons connected with the grazing system who have cattle on these grazing farms.'[30] Seven men from the Riverstown district, Andrew Flaherty, Charles Flaherty, John Ellis, John McMorrow, Denis Dowd, J. Sheeran and Michael Sheeran, were bound to the peace by the resident magistrate, F. B. Henn. After paying bail-money, however, the men were discharged. There was a growing sense of frustration among the police at the failure of the justice system in the county to deal with the agitation and County Inspector Holmes gloomily concluded, in his report for June 1908, that 'the league machinery is most complete, & the law as administered by juries & local JPs is of course powerless to deal with it'.[31]

Tensions and ambiguities often existed at ground level within UIL branches and, as police discovered, south Co. Sligo was no exception: a bizarre situation emerged in the county as early as July 1908 whereby the cattle of several UIL members were not only driven but that the owners themselves had participated in the process.[32] The South Sligo UIL executive did much to encourage the cattle-driving activity of its branches, passing resolutions in 'high appreciation' of the activities of the most active branches in the region which included those at Riverstown, Ballyrush and Kilcreevan.[33] Expectations of local land redistribution were heightened after John O'Dowd, MP, told an audience in Gurteen that the government would soon acquire 900,000 acres of untenanted land, under the much anticipated new land act, to distribute among the small farmers, labourers and farmers' sons.[34] According to the RIC County Inspector, James E. Holmes: 'the only thing thought of in the county dist[ricts] is the splitting up of the grazing lands & the most effective means of forcing legislation, regardless of the existing law.' Anxious to keep pressure on the government, it was little wonder that another clash with police occurred on

17 July 1908 when a patrol of two constables encountered a party of 40 men marching in fours and some in disguise, on their way to attempt a cattle-drive. The men 'ordered the police not to follow them & pelted them with stones till they found it prudent to withdraw'. The RIC County Inspector reported that the senior constable threatened to use his revolver and the cattle-drivers eventually dispersed, fearing that they would be identified or that police reinforcements might arrive; additional policemen had been drafted into the village, the police having received information that a raid for arms was planned on the Riverstown barracks.[35]

As noted, the Riverstown band was playing an increasingly active role in local UIL agitation. On one occasion, the band marched for four miles to parade around Major Eccles' meadow at Cams that a man named Bell was due to mow down the following day. After the band's visit, however, Bell refused to cut the meadow. Indeed, the band's influence was such that, as the County Inspector of the RIC reported in August 1908, it had been necessary to establish a second barracks in Riverstown 'chiefly on account of the disorderly & defiant behaviour of the local band' which was being 'used by the Riverstown br[anch] of the UIL as a means of intimidation'.[36] The nearby Sooey branch of the UIL was also cooperating with their local band in the enactment of anti-grazing agitation. On 12 August 1908, 12 people from that area were arrested and bound to good behaviour for their role in attempting to intimidate the holder of a grazing farm.[37] On Sunday 30 August 1908, the police were caught unawares by a 'hazel brigade' (so-called because the cattle-drivers tended to carry hazel sticks to drive the cattle) comprising the Riverstown, Ballyrush and Kilcreevan bands along with a large contingent of supporters, who turned up in Ballymote and paraded the town. As the South Sligo executive of the UIL was meeting in the town on the same day an impromptu demonstration was held and addressed by members of the executive including John O'Dowd, MP, John Gilmartin and C.W.P. Cogan – all of whom condemned the grazing system in the locality.[38]

While the use of boycotting for the purposes of intimidation was widespread, a sectarian aspect to the practice developed in the Riverstown district in the period of the Ranch War. It was in the summer of 1908 that the police first became aware that members of the Riverstown UIL were calling on Protestants in the district to force them to join or subscribe to the league.[39] Those who refused were soon boycotted with blacksmiths refusing to shoe their horses and milk-carriers being forbidden to carry their milk to the creamery. To transport milk at the least expense, 20 or so neighbours usually grouped together and paid a carrier/s to transport the milk at the rate of one farthing per gallon. The carrier got a respectable wage while the farmers got their milk delivered at the lowest possible rate. The farmer also ensured that he could work at home at the busiest times of year when the volume of milk to be delivered was greatest. The refusal of the local milk-carriers to transport the Protestants' milk, however, was a particularly significant source of hardship to small farmers; many had not even a horse or a cart to undertake a journey of five or six miles to the creamery.[40] Alfred George Elliott, the Church of Ireland bishop of Kilmore, Elphin and Ardagh, lamented: 'Our farmers where the law of the league prevails are placed in a dilemma – persecution on the one hand and demoralization on the other'.[41]

The boycott extended beyond farmers to Protestant shopkeepers in Riverstown whose trade was affected by a decline in Catholic customers. However, as the County Inspector of the RIC reported, the power of the UIL was such that Protestants who were boycotted admitted being 'afraid to give evidence for a prosecution'.[42] Moreover, those who dared to associate with boycotted Protestants were brought before the branch and compelled to promise to have no further contact; this fate befell an unnamed member of the Ballyrush UIL branch who assisted Edward Harte of Whitehill.[43] A member of the neighbouring Riverstown UIL, who carried the family of the Protestant rector to Ballymote in his car on 3 August 1908, was also called before his branch to account for his actions and to vow not to do so again. The Ballyrush UIL branch even went so far as to publish in the *Sligo Champion* the names of Protestant non-leaguers and called on people to note who they were and to act accordingly.[44] The unionist *Sligo Independent* newspaper considered it 'extraordinary that such intimidation and terrorism should be permitted and winked at by the government'.[45]

While the government was slow to respond to the various forms of agitation, the Roman Catholic Church became particularly vocal in its condemnation of boycotting. On Sunday 23 August 1908, the parish priest of Riverstown, Canon John Meagher, 'condemned in very strong language from the pulpit, the boycotting in general & of Protestants in particular' being carried out by the Riverstown UIL branch. Canon Meagher believed that the majority of Catholics were opposed to this practice and called on them to have the 'courage to put it down'.[46] His words had little effect though and the boycotting of Protestants farmers continued with shops in Riverstown refusing to deal with them. Even bakery firms in Sligo town, approximately 12 miles away, were afraid to supply bread owing to the influence of the UIL, which was now 'feared by all classes' in the region.[47]

In September 1908, the sectarian nature of the boycotting in the Riverstown district began to cause concern among some of the leading nationalists in the county, particularly after the appearance in the *Sligo Champion* of a letter written by Bridget King, of Drumfin, which described how her son William, a blacksmith and a member of the Kilcreevan UIL branch, was being boycotted because he continued to work for Protestants who had refused to join or subscribe to the league. With her son's trade badly damaged, Bridget King threatened to take legal proceedings against members of the Kilcreevan branch and the possibility arose that the *Sligo Champion* might also be sued. An editorial in the newspaper, which the police believed were the words of the editor, P.A. McHugh, MP, condemned the attempts to force Protestants to join the league and described the state of affairs as 'shocking'.[48] The police suspected that, apart from the threat of a civil action, McHugh's editorial may have been motivated by other factors including his candidature for the vacant post of secretary to the county council. The police believed that he may have received a letter on the matter from the Roman Catholic bishop of Elphin, John Joseph Clancy, who had been petitioned by Bridget King. McHugh may also have been acting under direct orders from the IPP, who vehemently opposed attempts to force Protestants to join the UIL against their will.

Whatever his reasons, McHugh now condemned the boycotting of Protestants, even though his newspaper played a pivotal role in reinforcing this tactic by regularly publishing resolutions passed by local UIL branches.[49] At a large UIL meeting held at Sooey, on 27 September 1908, both McHugh and his parliamentary party colleague, O'Dowd, warned their audience not to engage in the practice.[50] Having already defied the dictates of the Catholic parish priest, Canon Meagher, only time would tell whether or not the warnings of McHugh and O'Dowd would be heeded at Riverstown.

2. The shooting of John Stenson and its aftermath

In his monthly report for October 1908, RIC County Inspector James E. Holmes noted that 'the league agitation at Riverstown' was 'demoralising the neighbourhood' and that the area 'could hardly be in a more lawless condition'. Police patrols were nightly encountering groups of men on the roads, often armed with revolvers, on their way to drive cattle off grazing farms in the district. Shots were regularly heard at night by police patrols who noted that people appeared to be 'well armed with revolvers'. On the night of 14 October 1908, for example, the police heard a shot fired and arrested two men, whose boots and trousers were soaked wet, not far from grazing farms where the cattle had just been driven. Later that same night a third man was arrested with a loaded revolver and spare cartridges were found in his pockets. The three men appeared before the resident magistrate who discharged them without any 'recognizance for good behaviour' since the police could not prove they actually participated in a cattle-drive. According to County Inspector Holmes the 'people concluded from this that there was no risk in carrying revolvers, & they became more aggressive in their demeanour towards the police'.[1]

Further conflict looked inevitable when a cattle-drive at Riverstown was organized for 22 October 1908 and 'gallons of whiskey' were provided to the cattle-drivers 'to buck them up & give them courage to face the police'. Although the police report did not record who provided the whiskey, it may well have been the president of the Riverstown UIL branch, Thomas J. Judge, whose family had a licence to sell alcohol. Because only 80 men assembled for the drive, one of the secretaries of the UIL branch decided to cancel it as he felt that over 100 men would be necessary for the job. Although the police did not identify the secretary who called off the drive, it was most likely to have been Peter McGoldrick. He no longer signed off on branch notes published after this time and his perceived lack of initiative even seems to have led to his temporary expulsion from the Riverstown UIL branch.[2] The branch was becoming more extreme in its outlook, as evidenced by the following notice published in the *Sligo Champion* on 24 October 1908:

> The branch wish to call the attention of the young men in the district to the fact that the police have no right to stop and question them as to their whereabouts at any time, either day or night, such conduct being

simply pure bluff. Neither have the police any right to enter houses without a regular search warrant, or even to come to any houses demanding to know if any members of the family are absent or at home. There is no truth in the statement that police can stop people after 10 o'clock or at any time.[3]

The publication of such notices was now causing concern for the Liberal government who warned a number of local newspapers, throughout Ireland, that proceedings would be taken against them to prevent the publication of resolutions of an 'intimidatory character' passed by local UIL branches. On 28 October 1908, RIC District Inspector Brownrigg called to the offices of the *Sligo Champion* and served a notice to the editor, P.A. McHugh, MP, regarding the publication of 'intimidatory' resolutions. A similar notice was served to the editor of the *Roscommon Herald*, ex-MP Jasper Tully, warning that a prosecution would ensue if the paper continued to publish resolutions intended to intimidate the holders of grazing land.[4]

Notwithstanding the intervention of the government, tensions continued to escalate in the Riverstown district. At about 12.30 a.m. on the morning of 29 October a crowd of over 100 men marched into Riverstown, from the Cooper's Hill direction, past the police barracks and entered a grazing farm on the outskirts of the village held by Owen Phibbs, DL, of Seafield. As the farm had been 'driven' before and no attempt had been made to hide the preparations for that night's cattle-drive, Head Constable Donovan and ten other policemen were already on the farm to prevent it. Attempts by the police to get the crowd to withdraw proved futile and confrontation quickly developed with stones being thrown at the police, a wall built of loose stones by the side of the field providing plenty of ammunition. A number of policemen were struck by stones and shots were fired from the crowd. The *Sligo Independent* quoted an unnamed constable who recounted that 'the air was red with flashes' while the *Freeman's Journal* reported how 'neighbours' said that revolvers were fired by the crowd followed by the 'heavy ring of the police carbines'.[5] Head Constable Donovan was struck on the forehead by a stone and knocked to the ground whereupon rising he gave the order to fire. When the crowd eventually dispersed, the police came across the body of a young man named John Stenson lying on his back beside the stone wall. He was 19 years old and this was his first and only cattle-drive.[6]

On the evening of 28 October 1908, Stenson, who was employed as a labourer by a Protestant farmer named John Milliken, who lived nearby at Rusheen, had wandered into Riverstown after work to purchase some tobacco. Although Stenson was a Roman Catholic, it appears that he was not a member of any UIL branch in the county. It was later reported that, as both of his parents were deceased, a 70-acre farm was being held in trust for him in his native Tubbercurry until he came of age. Undoubtedly, the social nature of the planned cattle-drive and the sense of camaraderie it instilled, not to mention the prospect of outwitting the police, excited the interest of young men like John Stenson who was persuaded to remain on in Riverstown village for the event. However, it may well have been that Stenson's participation owed more to peer pressure given that, as already mentioned, a perceived shortage of manpower had caused the recent cancellation of at least one cattle-drive in Riverstown.

Stenson's body was removed to Riverstown courthouse where an inquest was held at 3 p.m. on 30 October 1908 by Dr Robert G. Roe, coroner for the district. A jury was sworn in and RIC District Inspector Francis Comerford represented the crown while the Sligo solicitor, Hubert Tully, represented Stenson's next of kin. The inquest was strictly confined to ascertaining the cause of death and any attempts to deviate from this purpose were prevented by Dr Roe who felt that such matters were 'more for a magisterial investigation.' Aside from the medical evidence and that of Stenson's employer, John Milliken, who confirmed the identity of the body, the only other evidence that was permitted was that of Sergeants Patrick McHugh and Thomas Durkan. No evidence was given by those who had participated in the cattle-drive. In his evidence, Sergeant McHugh described how he had gone to the grazing farm at 10.30 p.m. armed with a revolver while his colleague Constable McNamara carried a carbine. About an hour later they were joined by Head Constable Donovan, Sergeant Durkin, Acting-Sergeant Gray and Constables Scott, Quinn, Reilly, Calnan, McConville and Coulter bringing the total number of police in the field to eleven. At 12.30 a.m., they heard the sound of men marching on the road and subsequently a crowd entered the field and attempted to drive the cattle. McHugh also explained how it was a starlit night and that visibility was approximately 300 yards. Upon being ordered to leave the field by Head Constable Donovan and Sergeant Durkan the crowd responded by shouting at the police and throwing a volley of stones. Many of the police were struck with McHugh being hit in the chest. He recounted how he heard a voice shout 'fire on them [meaning the police]', while all the time the crowd grew more aggressive and began to close in on them. A shot was fired from the crowd at this stage. Head Constable Donovan was struck with a stone on the forehead and remained on the ground for some time but when he recovered he gave the order for the police to load their weapons. McHugh believed that their 'lives were in imminent danger' at that point and following further stone-throwing and shots from the crowd Head Constable Donovan gave the order to fire. The shots appeared to have little effect on the crowd who forced the police further back across the field. In his evidence, McHugh acknowledged that, at this point, 'we well understood that we were to fire at the crowd that was attacking us.' After further exchanges of fire, some of the crowd retreated back across the stone wall but returned when someone called out: 'Come back you cowards.' After the crowd eventually dispersed, the police found the body of John Stenson, lying on his back near the wall, with his head inclined to the right, blood on his face and a wound on the right side of this nose.[7]

Sergeant Durkan's evidence was quite similar and he agreed with Sergeant McHugh about revolver fire coming from the crowd. He had also been struck by a stone and he corroborated McHugh's testimony about hearing a shout from the crowd to open fire on the police. The only other evidence given was by Dr Edward King Frazer, the medical officer at Riverstown dispensary. Having carried out the post-mortem on the body, Dr Frazer concluded that Stenson had died from a gunshot wound to the head either from a revolver, rifle or other firearm. The bullet, which had not been recovered, entered between the bridge of the nose and the right eye and exited just behind the right ear. The jury agreed with Dr Frazer's analysis that death had been the result of a bullet wound which caused a 'laceration of the brain.'[8] It was rumoured that other members of the crowd had been wounded as a result of the confrontation with the police; the County Inspector of the RIC believed that two men were injured but he could not confirm it.[9] It was later revealed that the police had, in total, fired 18 shots from their carbines and five revolver shots during the course of the engagement.[10]

With tensions heightened following the fatality, an attempt to attack the RIC barracks in Riverstown was planned for the night of 30 October, but this did not go ahead after an intervention by Canon Meagher. Further trouble threatened to flare up on 31 October, the day of Stenson's funeral in Tubbercurry, when a revolver was produced by one of the returning Riverstown party in the presence of the RIC County Inspector Holmes. That evening, the secretary of the South Sligo UIL executive, John Gilmartin, gave an inflammatory speech which, according to Holmes, 'amounted to incitement to murder H[ea]d Cons[table] Donovan & the police'. The crowd at the meeting were disorderly and the situation looked to be deteriorating after one man threatened to shoot at the police with his revolver. District Inspector Francis Comerford was forced to bring out all his available men, armed with rifles, before the crowd broke up with one man on horseback hitting the RIC barracks with a stone before departing. While the County Inspector of the RIC disparagingly referred to Gilmartin as 'a drunken cobbler', he did acknowledge that his 'word was law in Ballymote' and that he was doing a great amount of harm.[11] An editorial in the *Sligo Independent* alleged that it was agitators like Gilmartin who were largely responsible for misleading the young men around Riverstown and that their 'folly had been sealed in blood and sudden death'. The newspaper claimed that on the night of Stenson's death the fighting was done by the 'rank and file' while the 'leaders' were safely

3 John Stenson's grave
in Rhue cemetery,
Tubbercurry.

ensconced in their own homes. The newspaper also lamented that the 'stirring up of bigotry' had caused 'strife, unrest, and hatred' in the once peaceful district of Riverstown.[12]

Other local newspapers, including the *Roscommon Herald,* reported that there was considerable exasperation among the young men of the Riverstown district over the 'way in which they alleged they were neglected by the MP's for the county'.[13] Neither John O'Dowd nor P.A. McHugh, both of whom seem to have initially underestimated the strength of local feeling about the incident, had come to Riverstown when the shooting occurred; neither had they attended the inquest or Stenson's funeral. O'Dowd's excuse that he was ill carried little weight and a crowd returning from the funeral stopped outside his residence in Bunninadden where they reportedly 'indulged in an extraordinary outburst of rage at his house, groaning and booing and the proceeding created a tremendous sensation'.[14] Sparked into action by this demonstration, O'Dowd's parliamentary colleague, P. O'Brien, questioned the chief secretary of Ireland, Augustine Birrell, about the Riverstown cattle-drive fatality in the house of commons on 5 November 1908. Birrell stated that he was satisfied with the inquest and that there was no intention to hold any further inquiry. Many nationalists, however, who felt aggrieved by the limited nature of the inquest and the fact that the only evidence accepted had been that of the police, were intent on obtaining a public inquiry. The increasing national significance of the incident also led to the intervention of the chairman of the IPP, John Redmond, who questioned the assertion that the crowd had used firearms on the night in question. Birrell responded by stating:

> I have to deal with a small force of policemen, eleven men in all, who appeared to have behaved with great discretion and to have been completely under command. They only fired at the command of their officer, and they tell me, without any hesitation or doubt, that the firing proceeded from the crowd at first. I cannot doubt that they are correct in that view, and I cannot see how you could obtain evidence of such a kind as to affect the merit and force of their evidence.[15]

Nevertheless, the incident at Riverstown put Birrell under increased pressure to put the Criminal Law and Procedure (Ireland) Act, 1887 (Crimes Act), or 'coercion' as it was more commonly known, into operation in counties such as Sligo. Under this act, which had been revoked by the Liberal administration soon after coming into office in February 1906, resident magistrates were given the powers of 'investigation and summary jurisdiction', while the lord lieutenant of Ireland could suppress a subversive organization.[16] Unionists such as the MP for Mid Armagh, John Lonsdale, pressed Birrell on the issue of law and order in the west of Ireland arguing that stronger measures needed to be taken against the cattle-drivers.[17] Sympathetic newspapers like the *Sligo Independent* reported that 'life had been made a veritable hell' for 'unionists' in Riverstown who were being victimized on account of their religious and political convictions.[18] Indeed, the tragedy had caused such a sensation that the *Times* believed that the incident threatened to cause a ministerial crisis with a section of the cabinet thought to be in favour of reinforcing the Crimes Act.[19]

   Irish unionists were not alone in their concern about lawlessness in the west of Ireland. Canon Meagher, the Roman Catholic parish priest of Riverstown, had taken a strong line against boycotting, cattle-driving and the other forms of intimidation that had occurred in the area, while the church hierarchy voiced its opposition to cattle-driving from an early stage. The *Irish Catholic* newspaper condemned it as a practice which 'could only have found its initiation in the maleficent mind of a semi lunatic and it says little for the intelligence or prudence of a section of our peasantry that they have been so foolish as to participate in it. 'The Liberal government was also reproached for inactivity which resulted in a 'state of social anarchy now prevailing in many portions of our western counties'. As well as holding the government responsible for the tragedy of John Stenson's death, the newspaper was fiercely critical of those who had involved the young man in their activities:

DESPERATE REMEDIES.

THERE WAS AN OLD MAN WHO SAID, "HOW
SHALL I STOP THE PURSUIT OF THAT COW?
I WILL SIT ON THIS STILE
AND CONTINUE TO SMILE."
(BUT IT GAVE NO RELIEF TO THE COW.)

4 Caricature of the chief secretary, Augustine Birrell, ignoring cattle-driving
in Ireland. Source: *Punch*, 18 Dec. 1907.

His [Stenson's] presence at the scene of conflict was due to the
thoughtlessness of youth rather than any feelings of malice towards others
… The same thing, however, cannot be said of the miscreants who
tempted him to his fate. These folk are now endeavouring to create the
impression that the constabulary are to blame for having fired when they
did. The truth, however, is that they would have been really to blame if
they had not fired, whereas now they are not deserving of censure but
of praise for creditable discharge of duty.[20]

Aside from dealing inadequately with the congested areas of the west, the other
major complaint against the government was that they had allowed the Peace
Preservation (Ireland) Act of 1881, better known as the Arms Act, which
regulated the sale and importation of arms, to lapse on 31 December 1906.
Under this act, no one in a district which had been 'proclaimed' could carry
arms or ammunition without authorization, while the police could search,
without a warrant, for arms and arrest anyone found with them in his
possession.[21] In the Riverstown district, the importation of arms and
particularly revolvers was so conspicuous that it came to the attention of the
Inspector General of the RIC, Neville Chamberlain. He reported, in
November 1908, that the president of Riverstown UIL, Thomas J. Judge,

supplied revolvers to people in the locality under an instalment system whereby the purchaser made a weekly payment until the total was paid off.[22]

In late October 1908, the government finally decided to take action against those involved in the boycotting of Protestants in Riverstown. Reports that the 'Riverstown conspiracy' case, as it became known, was a direct response to the cattle-drive at which John Stenson was shot, were shown by the *Roscommon Herald* to be undermined by the fact that the defendants' signatures on the summons predated the tragedy.[23] The defendants were summoned to appear at Riverstown petty sessions court on 5 November 1908 on charges of conspiracy to compel 15 Protestants, against their will, to join the UIL and to subscribe to its funds. The defendants, represented by the Sligo solicitor, M.J. Howley, were all from the Riverstown district and most gave their occupations as 'farmer' or 'farmer's son'. There were also blacksmiths, labourers, a tailor, a victualler and a builder (see Appendix B).[24] The most high-profile members of the local UIL branch to be charged were the vice-president, Thomas O'Gara and the deputy vice-president, John McDermott, while James Kerins, Edward McDonagh, James Sheerin, Martin Ellis, Bryan Flannery, Patrick Sweeney and Charles O'Hara, all served on the branch committee. In February 1909, the cases against Patrick Walsh, Charles Cawley and Mark Candon, the latter two being members of the branch committee, were struck out 'owing to illness' and the case against Henry King was withdrawn.[25]

The president of the Riverstown UIL branch, Thomas J. Judge, was conspicuously absent from the list of those accused due, presumably, to a lack of evidence of his participation. He tended to work at home and it appears that he did not venture out on the cattle-drives or band parades in the locality, thus limiting his direct involvement in the agitation. Although the police were certain that Judge was behind all the disturbances in Riverstown they found it extremely difficult to obtain tangible evidence against him and found that while the local Catholic clergy and the 'respectable inhabitants' of Riverstown disapproved of the disturbances in their locality, they were 'all afraid of Judge'.[26] Moreover, the police believed that while the 'respectable class' in Riverstown would be delighted if the leaders of the local branch were put in jail, they lacked the 'moral courage' to stand up to the UIL.[27] They had been reporting for some time that the Riverstown UIL seemed 'to possess more influence than any other' branch in south Sligo because they maintained an extreme outlook. They also considered that the branch was governed by 'persons of no stake in the locality', that there was 'not a farmer of any substance' on the branch committee and that Judge, as president of the branch, kept a following largely through 'lavish hospitality' at the expense of his father, a publican and merchant.[28]

While people in Riverstown may have been fearful of opposing Thomas J. Judge there was no such fear in nearby Conway's Cross where, in late 1908, the local UIL branch became involved in a bitter dispute with the Riverstown branch. The principal protagonists were Judge and the secretary of Conway's Cross UIL, James Conlon. The dispute centred on the fact that Conlon had cattle grazing on the farm of a tenant at Ardagh, which left him open to accusations from the Riverstown UIL that he was a rancher profiting by the grazing system. According to the police there was an 'old spleen' between the two men and it was no surprise when the Riverstown branch used the *Sligo Champion* to call on Conlon to withdraw his stock. In retaliation, Conlon wrote to the newspaper and accused Judge of hypocrisy in ensuring that the police could not obtain goods anywhere in Riverstown, except in his shop, while condemning others for even speaking to a policeman. Conlon pointed to the fact that Judge was not among the defendants in the Riverstown conspiracy case and he openly suggested that Judge was a 'gaol spy'.[29] For good measure, he also referred to Judge as an 'old-time English soldier' and a 'bockahaun' who had been 'shot in the heel' while running away from the Boers when he was in South Africa fighting for the British.[30]

The Riverstown conspiracy case came before a number of magistrates at Riverstown petty sessions court on 5 November 1908. On the day, though, the resident magistrate, Captain Fitzpatrick, decided to adjourn the case, due to a great volume of other business and summoned all parties to appear again at Ballymote court a week later, on 12 November 1908. Before this decision was announced, however, it emerged that 15 Protestants, who had been called as witnesses for the government, had not attended at Riverstown because, according to their solicitor Alexander M. Lyons, 'they wished to protest in the very strongest manner against the action of the Irish executive in summoning them as witnesses in the case.'[31] The witnesses consisted of 12 men and three women and they were nearly all small farmers from the general district of Riverstown who, according to Lyons, had been subjected to 'a reign of terror, intimidation, and boycotting' (see Appendix C).[32] According to the solicitor-general of Ireland, Redmond Barry, none of them were graziers but, rather, 'belonged to an old stock, and in no sense could be regarded as importations into the country'.[33] The *Roscommon Herald* reported that having felt abandoned by the government the Protestant Mutual Defence Association of Riverstown and District, a 'purely passive resistance association', had been founded to help them to 'protect their lives, their family, and their property'. In a statement, which their solicitor later submitted to the press, the association protested that, until Stenson had been killed, the government had done nothing to deal with the state of affairs in Riverstown, despite knowing of the plight of Protestants:

> No real attempt has been made to protect the Protestants or to allow them the ordinary liberty of action to which a subject of the king is entitled; in fact the government considered it a trivial matter until blood

was shed. Now that life had been taken, the government draw these unfortunate Protestants into the arena after refusing for six long horrible months or at any rate neglecting to give them the protection and assistance to which they are, as loyal subjects, entitled to.[34]

The association stated that they had little faith in the government protecting them from the 'religious tyranny and oppression' of the UIL and called on their co-religionists in Britain as well as the 'so called Protestant parliament' to protect them and their property. Indeed, their statement went as far as to compare the situation in Riverstown with the actions of Catholics in France prior to the St Bartholomew's Day massacre of Protestants in 1572. Significantly, the authorities believed that the real reason that the Riverstown witnesses adopted their course of action was actually 'for the purpose of disarming resentment against them'.[35]

Before the conclusion of proceedings at Riverstown petty sessions on 5 November 1908, Alexander M. Lyons informed the resident magistrate that his clients would not voluntarily attend as witnesses at Ballymote court the following week. Consequently, warrants were issued to ensure that they would be legally bound to attend. Once the proceedings had concluded, John O'Dowd, MP, attempted to put forward a resolution before the court in connection with the shooting of John Stenson. O'Dowd was a local magistrate, or judicial officer, who worked under the guidance of the resident magistrate and, although local magistrates did not necessarily have any legal qualifications, they could put forward cases for trial before a judge and jury. Captain Fitzpatrick refused to have anything to do with O'Dowd's request and left the bench along with a number of the other magistrates. O'Dowd, however, still managed to pass a resolution calling for a public inquiry into the circumstances of John Stenson's death, having acquired the support of six other magistrates including Anthony O'D. Cogan, James Hannan, John Cryan, William Robert McLoghry, James D. O'Brien and P.J. Flynn, the chairman of Sligo Rural District Council.[36]

Despite continual calls for a public inquiry into the shooting of Stenson, by Sligo County Council and other bodies, the Liberal government refused to grant an investigation. John O'Dowd, MP, argued, in the house of commons, that a number of witnesses had been prevented from giving evidence at the inquest in Riverstown and claimed that the general expectation had been that there would be an official inquiry, the delay in which had created speculation that the police actually had orders to fire on the people. While the chief secretary, Augustine Birrell, still considered an inquiry unnecessary he did consent to send someone to the district to make discreet inquiries.[37] Birrell later told the house of commons that those inquiries had revealed that the police behaved with discretion and were under control on the occasion. As regards other witnesses, he explained how the coroner gave the representatives of the next of kin ample opportunity to produce any evidence that they wished and denied that the coroner had said there would be a magisterial investigation.[38]

With the attention of the national press now firmly focused on Riverstown, a special correspondent from the *Irish Times* visited the area and interviewed a Protestant, who while wishing to remain anonymous explained how 'violence … was staring us in the face from the moment of our refusal to yield to the demands of the United Irish League.' It was also explained that the Protestant Mutual Defence Association had been founded shortly after the boycotting started in order for members to assist one another with farm work and other daily arrangements. By organizing in this way they had managed to get by and protect themselves from what the interviewee called the 'tyranny of the United Irish League.' The *Irish Times* correspondent was also informed that some of the more 'respectable Catholics' in the area had expressed their sympathy with the members of the Protestant association in their attempts to protect their liberties. The interviewee was anxious that peace would be restored to the district and expressed hope that Catholics would make an honest attempt to settle the whole matter amicably, with the support of their clergy.[39] Alexander M. Lyons, the association's legal representative, reiterated the desire for peace and stressed that despite intense provocation his clients had never 'attempted any retaliation by act or word'.[40] This was notwithstanding the fact that the UIL influence was now such that even the employees of the Anglo-American Oil Company had refused to supply Protestant shopkeepers in Riverstown with oil, presumably for paraffin lamps and other forms of lighting and heating, until the company's head office intervened. Likewise, the travelling carts of shopkeepers as distant as Sligo town and Dromahair, Co. Leitrim, had refused to supply bread with one bread-cart driver at Riverstown being 'threatened with death' by men in disguise. According to Lyons, all social contact between Protestants and Catholics had ceased and Protestants feared to go out after dark alone, unless armed or accompanied by friends.[41]

RIC anxiety over the lawless condition of the Riverstown district was manifested in elaborate precautions taken when Head Constable Donovan, who had been in charge the night Stenson was shot, travelled to Belfast in early November 1908. Extra police drafted into Riverstown were armed with double-barrel shotguns instead of the regular carbines.[42] The *Sligo Independent* reported that the railway tracks for two miles either side of Ballymote station were patrolled by plain-clothes RIC men and that a large number of constables accompanied Donovan to the station. Six plain-clothes policemen travelled on with him as far as Collooney to ensure his safety. Although nothing eventful occurred, these precautions were indicative of the heightened state of vigilance now adopted by the police.[43]

On the morning of 12 November 1908, the police removed a black flag which had been raised over Ballymote courthouse and white-washed over the words 'Remember Stenson' that had been painted in black on the building. Once the Riverstown conspiracy case hearing resumed there later in the day, the defendants' solicitor, M.J. Howley, requested, on behalf of his clients and on behalf of the Catholic parish priest of Riverstown, that the case be adjourned for three months. Howley argued that since there was now a 'great anxiety in the locality' for peace, especially after the death of John Stenson, the immediate pursuit of the case would only reignite bitterness and political feeling. He proposed that if the hearing was postponed for a period and the land bill promised by the government was introduced, 'all causes of unrest would disappear'. The crown objected to Howley's application and called on those magistrates who were members of the UIL not to adjudicate given their obvious partiality. None of the ten magistrates stepped down, however, and it was decided, on a majority of seven votes to three, that the case would be adjourned until 3 February 1909.[44]

3. The 'Riverstown conspiracy' case

Pending the resumption of the Riverstown conspiracy case in early 1909, the fate of John Stenson and the circumstances of his death would be exploited by various individuals, among them leading nationalist politicians ranging from the moderate to the extreme. Tensions relating to the Riverstown situation had surfaced within the IPP in November 1908 when the Riverstown UIL branch brought Jasper Tully, the independent nationalist editor of the *Roscommon Herald* and Laurence Ginnell, the MP for North Westmeath, to assist the defence in the conspiracy case hearing at Ballymote. According to the RIC County Inspector Holmes, this was a calculated move on the part of the Riverstown UIL made 'with the intention of unseating O'Dowd MP at the next election'. Although it had been stated in local newspapers that Ginnell would be employed in the defence of the UIL members, he did not actually attend proceedings on 12 November despite being in Ballymote on the day. Holmes recounted what had happened:

> Tully & Ginnell, the president of the Riverstown league (Judge) & some of the defendants were for fighting the case, but the local clergy & Messrs McHugh & O'Dowd MPs were in favour of applying for an adjournment. A prolonged & heated discussion took place, and Tully & Ginnell were routed, an application to adjourn for 3 months was made by defendants' solicitor, the magistrates, by a majority granted it ... This was a shock to the influence of the extreme party at Riverstown & Ballymote.[1]

It appears that McHugh and O'Dowd, the two sitting IPP MPs for the county, forcefully asserted their control and, backed by the Catholic clergy, overrode the wishes of Ginnell, Tully and the more 'extreme' nationalists in the district.

The *Roscommon Herald* considered that attempts had been made to 'hush up the whole business' and that the Liberal government, fearful of Ginnell 'making the country ring with his denunciations of the [Stenson] tragedy', effectively pressurized their IPP allies to 'muzzle' him. The newspaper also reported that O'Dowd and McHugh had told defendants that unless Ginnell stepped aside they would withdraw all the nationalist magistrates from the bench at Ballymote courthouse thus ensuring that the case would be automatically sent forward for trial by a judge and jury.[2] Significantly, the authorities considered this to be an empty threat, believing that the IPP would be 'most unwilling' that 'there should be any public proof of sworn evidence that Protestants were being treated as alleged'.[3] The evidence given by witnesses during the Riverstown conspiracy case hearing, however, would not only provide 'public proof' of the treatment of Protestants in south Sligo during the Ranch War but also reveal much about the methods of the UIL in the area.

Though he was prevented from assisting the defendants at Ballymote, Laurence Ginnell's interest in events at Riverstown did not diminish. In the house of commons he took any opportunity to make reference to Riverstown and, on one occasion, accused the Protestant Mutual Defence Association of intimidating Protestants in Riverstown to force them to switch their trade from Catholic to Protestant traders, and of creating the ill-will in the area which had 'recently eventuated in murder.'[4] On another occasion, Ginnell seized on the contents of a telegram that the Inspector General of the RIC, Neville Chamberlain, had sent to the District Inspector at Ballymote after the tragedy at Riverstown which read:

> Please inform Head-Constable Donovan and the men who under his command repelled the attack on the police of an armed party of cattle-drivers, in the early morning of the 29th inst., that I am grateful to learn how well they upheld the traditions of the force on that occasion. I much regret to learn that Head-Constable Donovan was injured. Please inform me how he is.[5]

Albeit a personal message, Chamberlain's telegram angered many nationalists due to the absence of any mention of John Stenson and the reference to upholding the 'traditions of the force' in an incident where a youth had been shot dead by police. Ginnell unsuccessfully called on the government to express their disapproval of the telegram as he felt that it provided encouragement for the police to fire at other cattle-drivers.[6]

Ginnell, who was later expelled from the IPP in 1910, was not slow to use the incident at Riverstown for his own objectives. At a UIL meeting in his own constituency at Delvin, Co. Westmeath, in early January 1909, he caused a commotion by holding up an empty cartridge which he informed his audience was 'the exploded cartridge with which John Stenson was murdered, and which was picked up at the ranches at Riverstown.'[7] Although it was highly unlikely that his claim was true, it still served as an important source of propaganda. Nationalists were not alone in realizing the political expedience of the Riverstown tragedy. At a speech given in England, in mid-November 1908, the marquess of Lansdowne, a unionist and Conservative member of the house of lords, used the situation in Riverstown to protest at the lax control over the importation of arms into Ireland. However, what was of even graver concern, in his opinion, was the continued effect of such incidents of lawlessness on what he called the 'loyal minority' in Ireland:

… it is not only the local importance of these events, it is the profound discouragement of those who remain loyal to our cause in Ireland, who see themselves deserted, and who, after all, being ordinary human beings, if they are deserted long enough will begin to feel they are playing a losing game which is scarcely worth while to go on playing.[8]

Lansdowne's words certainly echoed the sense of abandonment expressed by Protestant witnesses during the conspiracy case.

At the beginning of 1909, conditions in the Riverstown district began to improve somewhat. There were a number of reasons for this, among them the fact that because most of the grazing farms were not stocked, given the time of year, there was little or no cattle-driving. In addition, the IPP MPs for the county, P.A. McHugh and John O'Dowd, were advising the people of Sligo to give the chief secretary, Augustine Birrell, a chance to introduce a satisfactory land bill that would address the redistribution of untenanted land. Another factor may have been that Sligo County Council, chaired by John O'Dowd, had received a bill of £269 for extra police and RIC expenses for the period between 25 June and 30 September 1908 when the anti-grazing agitation was at its height.[9] Thus, as the police observed, the Riverstown UIL branch was on 'its best behaviour pending the adjourned hearing of the Riverstown conspiracy prosecution'.[10]

The Riverstown conspiracy case began in earnest on 3 February 1909 with a hearing at the petty sessions court in Riverstown. The key issue for the magistrates to decide upon was whether or not there was sufficient evidence to send the defendants forward for trial. The solicitor for the crown prosecution, Dudley White, argued that the witnesses' testimony showed clear evidence of a 'combination' to force Protestants to support the Riverstown UIL. Several witnesses described how, after refusing the approaches of various members of the Riverstown branch to join the UIL or to pay a subscription, their usual milk-carriers refused to take their milk to Riverstown creamery. One of the witnesses, James Johnston (senior) of Drumfin, told the court how he had employed one of the defendants, William Tonry, to take his milk to the creamery. When Johnston refused to subscribe to the UIL in June 1908, Tonry, a Catholic, informed him that he could no longer work for him. In August 1908, however, an aggrieved Tonry offered to carry Johnston's milk again informing him that 'Wm. King was working for Protestants, and that Mr Judge, of Riverstown, was giving goods to them, and that he ought to be allowed to earn money as well as they.'[11] After a few days, though, Tonry stopped carrying the milk and two workmen Johnston employed also refused to work for him any longer. James Johnston (junior) had encountered similar difficulties with his milk-carrier, Bernard Higgins, a Catholic neighbour, after refusing a request by William King and Matthew Morrison to subscribe to the UIL. Johnston (junior) explained that Higgins also asked him to subscribe, saying that 'he would not like to see a drum coming to' Johnston's 'door'.[12] (The 'drum' was a reference to the 'drumming parties' or parades carried out by the Riverstown band under the auspices of the local UIL branch.) Johnston was also a shoemaker by trade but had seen a considerable decline in his business with his Catholic customers having deserted him since the boycott began.[13]

Two other Protestant witnesses, Thomas Morrison and John Harte, recounted how William King, who was a blacksmith, refused to shoe horses for them as he feared that he might encounter difficulties with the creamery and his own milk if he did. (This was the same William King whose mother, Bridget, had written to the *Sligo Champion* in September 1908 about her son being boycotted for working for Protestants.) John Harte subsequently asked another of the defendants, Bernard McDermott, who was also a blacksmith, to shoe his horse. Although McDermott initially agreed, he refused the following day. On his third attempt John Harte eventually managed to get John Hannon to shoe his horse. Unfortunately for Hannon, his anvil was stolen as a consequence with the RIC County Inspector Holmes believing that it had been thrown in a lake.[14] Other Protestants who refused to join the league also suffered pecuniary loss. Margaret Rowlette put up eight acres of meadow for rent in the summer of 1908 but the auction was boycotted and only two Protestant neighbours turned up. She eventually rented it, at a loss of almost £10 compared to previous years, to a number of Protestant farmers. Elizabeth Meredith's milk-carrier refused to take her milk to the creamery and spikes were put in one of her meadows. Her brother's mowing machine was damaged and some of the cutters were broken as a result.[15]

Notwithstanding all of this testimony, the solicitor for the defendants, M.J. Howley, argued that although it was clear that milk had not been carried for certain Protestants there was no evidence of a conspiracy against them. The magistrates agreed and, by a majority of six to three, they decided against sending the conspiracy case forward for trial.[16] The two resident magistrates, F.B. Henn and Captain Fitzpatrick, both admitted in court that they had voted in the minority. Of the seven other magistrates, it was almost certainly Arthur Cooper O'Hara of Coopershill, Riverstown, who voted with Henn and Fitzpatrick. The impartiality of at least four of the six who voted in favour of the defendants is questionable given their associations: John O'Dowd, MP and James Hannan were chairman and treasurer, respectively, of the South Sligo executive of the UIL; John M. Cryan was treasurer of the Keash UIL branch; Anthony O'D. Cogan was the father of the UIL organizer, C.W.P. Cogan.[17] The final two magistrates were James D. O'Brien, Ballymote, a Catholic grazier and William Robert McLoghry, Carrickcoola, a Protestant farmer.[18] The presence of a significant number of UIL members among the magistrates did not go unnoticed and was criticized by Captain Bryan Cooper, a Sligo native and member of the Irish Landowners' Convention, who felt that these men 'had not done their duty'.[19] In the house of commons, Sir Edward Carson, the unionist MP for Trinity College Dublin, used the statement made by the Riverstown Protestant Mutual Defence Association in November 1908 to highlight the failure of the ordinary law in rural districts. He pointed out that the Protestants had testified in court, despite the threat of being 'marked', and decried the fact that, even though their evidence was not contradicted, the magistrates had refused to send the case forward for trial.[20]

Carson's observations on the lawless state of rural areas like Riverstown was given further credence by an attempt made to intimidate a police constable named Shivnan in February 1909. Shivnan, who gave evidence for the crown prosecution at Riverstown petty sessions, was the subject of a threatening notice, consisting of a coffin bearing the constable's name, which was sketched on a telegraph pole close to the RIC barracks in Riverstown.[21] The issue of law and order also remained a concern for the hierarchy of the Roman Catholic Church in Ireland. Alluding to the actions of the UIL at Riverstown in his Lenten pastoral letter for 1909, Bishop John Joseph Clancy of Elphin referred to the 'conduct of certain uncontrolled and irresponsible branches of the national organisation' which were demoralizing the people and ruining the country. Clancy informed Catholics that not only were the various forms of intimidation, such as cattle-driving, meadow-spiking and conspiracy to prevent someone exercising their legal rights, condemned by the church but they were also categorized as 'reserved sins'. This meant that they could not be dealt in the ordinary sacrament of confession and could only be dealt with by the bishop or his appointed representative. The pastoral letter also condemned the commission of perjury by jurors and witnesses at petty sessions and assizes which was highly significant given the fact that the Riverstown conspiracy case was still passing through the courts. Such pronouncements were clearly an attempt by the church to discourage cattle-driving and intimidation in the south Sligo region.[22]

Despite the local magistrates voting against sending the conspiracy case forward for trial, the crown prosecution was intent on pursuing the matter. Thus, the next phase of the Riverstown conspiracy case occurred at the Sligo spring assizes in March 1909 where the crown made an application to pursue the case not in Co. Sligo but in Co. Dublin. This application was largely based on an affidavit by RIC County Inspector Holmes, who stated that the presence of so many UIL members among the magistrates at Riverstown, as well as resolutions passed by local UIL branches in support of the defendants, and the great excitement and interest in the case throughout the region, meant that 'it would be impossible at present to obtain a fair and impartial trial of the accused.'[23] This was consistent with Holmes' own RIC report for March 1909 which described a story being circulated in Riverstown about the president of the UIL branch, Thomas J. Judge. Apparently, Judge had 'induced' the Protestant magistrate and farmer, William Robert McLoghry of Carrickcoola (who had voted against sending the conspiracy case forward for trial), to write to the chief secretary Augustine Birrell and request that the Riverstown case be dropped altogether. The appeal was evidently unsuccessful as a case hearing went ahead at the Sligo spring assizes, but another matter now came to light: the alleged canvassing of jurors. It was discovered that the jury panel had been privately published and distributed in order to influence jurors in the case of seven Geevagh men charged with riot and unlawful assembly; this was connected to the Riverstown conspiracy case as it was to be tried by the same panel on the same day. County Inspector Holmes reported that copies of the jury panel members were distributed by 'a journalist, a prominent member of the Sligo UIL', which may well have been a reference to the owner of the *Sligo Champion*, P.A. McHugh, MP. Holmes also stated that, in the days prior to the assizes, two men had visited the homes of several of the Protestant witnesses in the Riverstown case and got them to 'sign a blank paper, giving them to understand that it was to be affixed to a memorial to the Lord Lieut[enant], to stop the prosecution'.[24] In spite of the various efforts to thwart its progress, the Riverstown conspiracy case was brought before Justice Andrews at the Sligo spring assizes, who eventually agreed to adjourn the case to enable the crown to apply to the King's Bench Division for a change of venue. The request was granted on 30 April and the trial venue chosen was Co. Dublin.[25]

Thus, the Riverstown conspiracy case finally came to trial in May 1909 and was heard over two days before the lord chief justice of Ireland, Lord Peter O'Brien and a Co. Dublin jury. The counsel for the crown included the solicitor-general, Redmond Barry, MP, KC, Sergeant Moriarty and Dudley White (instructed by T.H. Williams) while the counsel for the defendants consisted of Patrick Lynch, KC (instructed by M.J. Howley). One of the defendants, William Tonry, decided to represent himself. Much of the first day was given over to the evidence against the defendants with accounts of the refusal of milk-carriers to take milk, the refusal of blacksmiths to shoe horses, the spiking of a meadow, the boycott of an auction of a meadow and the loss of labour. James Bright, one of the Protestants, also gave evidence that after refusing to join the league a Catholic mason, Thomas Mulligan, who was working on his house left his employment after being 'hooted' and shouted at. In court, Mulligan recounted how a crowd of approximately 30 people had come to his house one night at 12.45 a.m. and woke him up. They told him not to work for James Bright anymore and he promised that he would not. Later, he went before the Riverstown UIL branch to apologize for his conduct and, subsequently, the following document had been published in the *Sligo Champion*:

I the undersigned beg to offer my sincere apologies to the committees
of the Riverstown and Kilcreevan branches for the manner in which I
have infringed the rules of the UIL by working for objectionables, and
I hereby promise not to have any connection with such characters in
future. Signed, Thomas Mulligan.[26]

On the second day of the trial, the lord chief justice raised the point with
counsel that a number of the defendants appeared to be on friendly terms
with the Protestant prosecution witnesses. This was confirmed in evidence
given by individuals such as William Clifford who admitted that he and
William Tonry, one of the defendants who had stopped carrying his milk, were
'on the best of terms'. Margaret Rowlette also told the court that she and
Thomas O'Gara, another defendant, 'were always good friends'.[27] The lord
chief justice opined that the answer to this anomaly was that some of the
defendants had been 'coerced by the league' and acted as they did under duress.
Sergeant Moriarty, in his closing speech for the prosecution, touched on this
theme and referred in particular to the case of William Tonry: 'they could only
infer what kind of terrorism it was that prevailed in that [Riverstown] district
which induced a man of good character, the excellent antecedents, and kindly
feelings of Wm. Toury [sic] towards his neighbours, to give up performing the
acts by which he earned his livelihood'.[28] Moriarty argued that the Protestants
were not boycotted simply because of their religion but because they refused
to join the UIL. This pointed to the crown's motivation in pursuing the case:

> The object of the prosecution was not to punish these men, but to deter
> others in the country from entering into combinations and making the
> lives of their Protestant neighbours absolutely intolerable, as they would
> be, if this kind of thing were tolerated. What government could possibly
> tolerate such a condition of things as this?[29]

The charge against the defendants was that they had entered into a criminal
conspiracy to force a number of Protestants in the Riverstown district to join
or subscribe to the UIL. Thus, what the jury had to decide was whether or
not the defendants had acted in concert, whether or not there was an actual
organized conspiracy and if the actions outlined by the prosecution resulted
from the refusal of the Protestants to join or subscribe to the UIL. After
deliberating for two hours and twenty minutes the jury failed to reach a verdict
and were dismissed. Although the defendants were bound over to present again
for trial if called upon, this never happened and, on 2 March 1910, Redmond
Barry, now the attorney-general, informed Captain Bryan Cooper in the house
of commons that the government did not intend to pursue the case any
further.[30]

Back in Co. Sligo, the feud between the Conway's Cross and Riverstown UIL branches had escalated and policemen had been kept busy by attempts to drive cattle belonging to the Conway's Cross branch secretary, James Conlon, as well as 'drumming' by the local band near his house.[31] The dispute eventually came before the South Sligo executive of the UIL in early 1909 when the MP for North Sligo, P.A. McHugh, who appeared to be weary of the activities of the Riverstown UIL branch, denied the accusation that Conlon was a rancher.[32] According to police, it was now 'well known' McHugh 'did not approve of Judge's policy of disturbance at Riverstown'.[33] At a later meeting of the executive, tensions between the various factions boiled over and the chairman, the treasurer James Hannan, who chaired in the absence of John O'Dowd, MP, struggled to keep control. During the course of the meeting, P. Conry, who represented the Collooney branch, denied that the land Conlon rented was a grazing ranch and accused the 'officers of the Riverstown League of holding 11 months land in all quarters around Riverstown'.[34] Both Paul Bew and Alvin Jackson have identified the difficulties that the Ranch War created not only for the IPP but for the nationalist movement as a whole with a high proportion of the leaders of the agitation themselves being, or later becoming, graziers. This often led to the rather farcical position whereby 'graziers sat on public platforms denouncing the very system from which they were profiting'.[35]

Tensions within the IPP also manifested in relation to the fund-raising efforts of the Stenson memorial committee, which was set up in late 1908, under the chairmanship of Thomas J. Judge and consisted of UIL members from the Riverstown and surrounding branches. The Stenson memorial committee met regularly to co-ordinate the collection of funds to pay for a commemorative statue. Subscriptions to the commemorative fund were slow, though, something that the memorial committee attributed to the 'apathy of the press in not giving more publicity' to their funding appeals.[36] Jasper Tully and Laurence Ginnell, the MP for North Westmeath, who had both maintained a close interest in the events at Riverstown, contributed at an early stage as did certain IPP members outside of Co. Sligo, among them Thomas Kettle (East Tyrone), J.J. Shee (West Waterford), John Philips (South Longford), J.J. O'Kelly (North Roscommon) and John Dillon (East Mayo). However, as John Gilmartin, the secretary of South Sligo UIL executive, revealed, two 'unnamed members of the party' refused to contribute anything to the commemorative fund.[37] As already noted, there was a more moderate element within the IPP who were strongly opposed to the intimidatory strategies of the UIL and to what they perceived as an attempt by the Riverstown UIL to glorify the death of Stenson.[38] The police noted too that the 'better class of people take no active part in the movement.'[39] Thus, in March 1909, the memorial committee passed a resolution to request that the South Sligo executive of the UIL 'take more active steps' to ensure that branches submitted their collections promptly.[40]

One of the ways that Thomas J. Judge himself appears to have contributed to this effort was by realigning himself with the IPP. Until February 1909, Judge had been generally regarded as a 'Tullyite', particularly after his involvement in attempts to use the Riverstown conspiracy case to undermine John O'Dowd, the South Sligo MP. After attending a nationalist convention in Dublin, chaired by the IPP leader, John Redmond, in February 1909, Judge returned to mainstream nationalism. At a UIL meeting in Riverstown shortly afterwards, Judge proposed a number of resolutions repudiating more extreme nationalist elements, like Tully and Ginnell, and expressing confidence in the parliamentary party and its members in Sligo. The meeting was adjourned early due to a local funeral and none of the resolutions were actually put to the floor – but they are indicative of Judge's political journey.[41] Despite Judge's pronouncements, there were, by April 1909, growing concerns about the security situation around Riverstown particularly as the commencement of the grazing season drew near. The police observed that there was now 'a good deal of friction over the grazing farms in league circles' and believed that prominent UIL members were engaged in complicated manoeuvres to acquire land for themselves. They noted, in particular, that Judge intended to quietly take the stocking of a number of local farms until it became known that 'McDermott', a committee member of the branch, had arranged to take the Ardkeerin grazing farm on the outskirts of Riverstown village. Both men were shopkeepers and thus business rivals. The police expected trouble in the form of cattle-drives once McDermott stocked the farm and believed that Judge would be motivated to divert McDermott's customers to his own shop.[42]

Hostility was also beginning to mount against the RIC after news emerged of the promotion of Head Constable Donovan, who had been in charge on the night that John Stenson had been shot. Not only had Donovan been promoted but he had also received a first-class service record and a gratuity of £12 from the RIC authorities. The chief secretary of Ireland, Augustine Birrell, defended this action in the house of commons stating that Donovan had been rewarded for his 'courage, coolness, and determination on the occasion in question.'[43] Sligo Corporation responded by condemning the actions of the RIC authorities and passing the following resolution in protest:

> That the announcement publicly of the advancement, promotion and gratuity to Head Const. O'Donovan, who was in charge of a party of police at Riverstown when young Stenson was shot dead by the police, we consider an outrage on the feeling of the people of this district and all Ireland as a maladministration of justice and fair play administered by the head of police (Col. Chamberlain) who sent the noted telegram

... and we consider the administration, who can promote their satellites and policeman who was responsible for the loss of a young life, incapable and incompetent.[44]

Shortly afterwards, on the night of 20 May 1909, a three-man RIC patrol was accosted on the road between Riverstown and Ballymote by a group of 12 to 14 men who shouted 'Remember Stenson' and threatened to avenge his death. One of the men, Bernard Brady of Cloonlurg, boasted of having a revolver and 'knowing how to use it'. Constable Peter McCormack, Ballymote, recounted in court how John McGarrigle, Ardree, shouted 'We'll knock out of you what you did to Stenson' and 'Remember Riverstown and old Donovan'. Five of the men were later arrested but were simply bound over by the resident magistrate to be of good behaviour.[45] Hostility towards the police also extended to a 'section of young girls' in the locality who had been observed accompanying members of the force and whom the Stenson memorial committee suspected were passing information to the police about events in their area. At a meeting of the committee in August 1909, these women were condemned and the young nationalists of the district were called upon to take note of their behaviour.[46]

Aside from increasing the police presence in Riverstown, attempts were made throughout 1909 to deal with the root of the anti-grazing agitation in the district. Part of the Ardcumber grazing farm, for instance, was made available by the district council for the building of labourers' cottages; on 8 July 1909, approximately 100 men assembled to fence in the plots marked out for these cottages. The area where John Stenson was shot was also fenced in, pending the erection of a suitable monument.[47] In November 1909, the RIC County Inspector Holmes reported that three large grazing farms comprising 511 acres in the Ballymote police district, which included Riverstown and its environs, were to be divided up among the owners of uneconomic holdings and others.[48] The division of some of the untenanted grazing land in the area among labourers and small farmers undoubtedly went some way towards restoring peace to the district.

Conclusion

On 29 August 1909, the first of a series of public demonstrations, organized by the Stenson memorial committee and honouring the memory of John Stenson, took place at Rhue graveyard, Tubbercurry, Co. Sligo. The occasion involved the unveiling of a Celtic cross at Stenson's grave, followed by a public meeting. A special train ran from Collooney while 92 cars and two brakes made the journey by road in convoy. The public spectacle and theatre of the event was added to by the presence of bands that played a number of national airs as the occasion required. The inscription on the gravestone went as follows: 'Erected by the Irish people to the memory of John Stenson, aged 19 years, murdered by the armed hirelings of Dublin Castle, at Riverstown, on October 29th, 1908.' In his speech the UIL organizer, C.W.P. Cogan, boasted that 'he was the first cattle-driver who came to Riverstown, and the first to raise the banner, and urge the policy of cattle-driving in that district.' Other speakers included John O'Dowd, MP, who referred to Stenson as 'a martyr in the Land War' but perhaps the most interesting speaker was the secretary of Riverstown UIL, Thomas Cawley, who gave his version of events on the night that Stenson was shot.[1]

Cawley stated that cattle-driving was 'neither a sin or a crime' and that the cattle-drivers in the area were respectable 'tenant farmers and the sons of tenant farmers.' He told the crowd (estimated at between 5,000 and 6,000 people) that he had led the cattle-drivers on that night and he gave a very different version of events to that supplied by the police witnesses at the inquest. He outlined how a campaign of cattle-driving was planned during the months of May to October 1908 to secure the redistribution of the grazing ranches in the area. His version of the night's events went as follows: On the night of Stenson's death, a crowd of about 50 men marched to Owen Phibbs' grazing farm at Riverstown to scatter the cattle. On entering the field a police sergeant told them to 'go back or we'll blow your brains out; ye drove this farm before, but we'll make ye pay for it now.' While they contemplated how best to move the cattle, the police began to throw stones at them and a number of the crowd were injured. The crowd responded with a volley of stones, driving the police back and Head Constable Donovan was knocked down. Upon getting up, he gave the order to fire on the crowd. In Cawley's account, the crowd used no firearms but responded to the police fire with volleys of stones drawn from the stone wall. It was on a trip to the wall for more stones that Stenson was shot. Cawley believed that the police were frustrated at their inability to adequately counteract the cattle-driving agitation and as a consequence they were 'thirsting for blood, blood money and promotion.' Cawley explained that Stenson had been left in the field because when some of the crowd lit matches to try identify the body the police had fired upon them.[2] Following Cawley's speech, a pamphlet was printed and circulated by the *Sligo Champion* newspaper which gave this version of the events surrounding the death of John Stenson.[3]

On 31 October 1909, the foundation stone of the memorial to John Stenson was laid in Riverstown. The occasion, attended by contingents from Sligo, Roscommon, Leitrim and Mayo, provided a public forum for nationalists in the region to reaffirm their loyalty to John Redmond and the IPP and for the IPP to present a show of unity. Among the speakers at the event were the two MPs for Sligo, John O'Dowd and Thomas Scanlan (who had replaced P.A. McHugh after his death in 1909), as well as the MP for South Meath, David Sheehy. The 1909 land bill, which was then passing through parliament, featured prominently in their speeches while the breaking up of the grass ranches and the redistribution of untenanted land was deemed of vital importance. In his speech, O'Dowd promised that if the bill proved unsatisfactory 'they would start an agitation such as would shake the English government in Ireland to its foundations.' The secretary of the South Sligo executive of the UIL, John Gilmartin, was even more provocative and outlined to the audience how they should treat the 'landlords of the ranches' and those 'grabbers' who rented such grasslands:

> No law, human or divine, could compel a man to speak to another, and if they treated the grabber as an outcast he would very soon give up his ill-gotten goods and clear away (cheers). Shun the grabber as you would shun a plague-stricken city (cheers) and let him see that the people will not tolerate such conduct amongst them (cheers).[4]

The Riverstown conspiracy case received a mention from David Sheehy who referred to the Protestant Mutual Defence Association as the 'Association of Distressed Unionists'. In a clear reference to those who had refused to carry milk for Protestants he declared that he 'hoped they were not carrying the milk yet for them (cheers) and if such people asked them to carry their milk it was at their own risk they would carry it, for it might get spilt before it got to the creamery (loud cheers)'. Two days later, on 2 November 1909, the Protestant Mutual Defence Association heard an address from Captain Bryan Cooper at a meeting in Riverstown which was chaired by Arthur Cooper O'Hara of Coppershill. Cooper complemented the association 'on their pluck and endurance during the troubles they had so recently passed through' but warned them to remain organized in case there was a recurrence of their difficulties. Promising to be of any assistance that he could, both at home and abroad, Cooper also told his audience that Riverstown was 'an instance of how Protestants might hold out in other parts of Ireland'.[5]

A little over a year after the shooting at Riverstown, a solemn High Mass was held in Riverstown Catholic church for the repose of the soul of John Stenson and the memorial committee presented his sister, Kate, with a cheque for £50.[6] Despite some of the difficulties which had been encountered, £228 had been raised by the memorial committee at the end of July 1910; £100 of this came from south Sligo, £86 from America, £10 from Sligo town, Ballintogher, Collooney and Ballisodare, £7 from Scotland and England, £7 from towns in Leitrim and Roscommon, almost £7 from Co. Mayo, £6 from Craughwell, Co. Galway and the rest from north Sligo and elsewhere in Ireland. The death of John Stenson certainly struck a chord with the Irish diaspora in America, with subscriptions received from Philadelphia and Butte (Montana), as well as from organizations such as the Sligo Social Club of Boston and the Co. Sligo Men's Social and Benevolent Association of New York.[7] However, despite these contributions the memorial committee still found themselves in debt to the tune of almost £90 'owing to the apathy shown by professing nationalists', as the committee secretary, Thomas Cawley, outlined.[8]

Some of the general apathy towards the collection of funds by the memorial committee may have been the result of a persistent belief that Stenson had died as a result of 'drunken rowdyism and organised rowdyism'. At a meeting of the South Sligo executive of the UIL in July 1909, Cawley, who claimed to have led the men on the night in question, refuted the story that anyone had been under the influence of alcohol. Thomas J. Judge, whose term as Riverstown UIL branch president had ended in June, condemned the 'malicious and misleading' statements which he believed were circulated by 'graziers and grabbers'.[9] Throughout 1909 and 1910, letters continued to appear in various regional and national newspapers appealing for funds to help the memorial committee to clear the debt; the UIL organizer, C.W.P. Cogan, for example, appealed to the cattle-drivers and UIL branches of Co. Galway in the pages of the *Connacht Tribune* while a letter from Thomas Cawley appeared in the *Evening Telegraph*.[10]

Despite the financial difficulties, on 15 August 1910, a statue of John Stenson was officially unveiled at Riverstown on the spot where he had been shot; the statue, completed by J. Clarence of Ballysodare, was mounted on a limestone pedestal. What might otherwise have been a significant local event was brought to the national stage by the presence of John Dillon and the involvement of the IPP. The unveiling was well attended, with numerous contingents from the surrounding counties, accompanied by bands gathering for the ceremony which was carried out by Dillon. In his speech, he disagreed with those who condemned the practice of cattle-driving regarding it 'as the natural outbreaking of the people against an abominable system of extermination which has depopulated and laid waste the most fertile and fairest lands of Ireland and drove the people to madness.'[11] While Dillon had made few previous utterances on the shooting of John Stenson he now reiterated the call for the government to grant a full public inquiry.[12] With the second general election of 1910 due in December, political opponents such as the independent nationalist, Maurice Healy, were quick to respond to Dillon's Riverstown speech. Healy dismissed Dillon's new found approval of the cattle-drivers and made the point that Dillon and the IPP were now supporting the very government and minister, chief secretary Augustine Birrell, that Dillon had criticized for not granting a public inquiry at Riverstown.[13] Indeed, the inscription on the base of the statue left little doubt over who the memorial committee blamed for the death of John Stenson:

> Erected by the Irish people and their exiled brethren of New York, Boston, Philadelphia and Butte Montana in memory of John Stenson who when striving in the cause of the land for the people was murdered on this spot by the order of Dublin Castle on 29th Oct. 1908.

In many ways, the district of Riverstown can be regarded as a microcosm of Irish rural society and the challenges it faced in the early 20th century. This study has investigated how the anti-grazing agitation known as the Ranch War operated at local level in Co. Sligo by focusing primarily on the activities of the Riverstown UIL branch. Some of the major issues in Irish society at the time were played out at local level in Riverstown: the debate over law and order and the call for coercion to be reintroduced; the importation and distribution of guns following the lapse of the Arms Act; the tensions created in the nationalist movement by the Ranch War agitation; the emergence of a more extreme form of nationalism; unionist concerns over the fate of the loyal Protestant minority in the west of Ireland. Unlike many of the activities in which the Riverstown UIL branch engaged, the campaign against the local Protestants was not about land. Nearly all of the Protestant witnesses that were called in the conspiracy case were small farmers and none of them appeared to have been graziers. Was the motivation behind it simply about gathering more funds or was there an element of social control involved? Was the campaign intended to cow the local Protestants who not only differed in religion but also in politics from their Catholic neighbours?

Although Protestants were the subject of a campaign of intimidation the evidence suggests that there was not any deep-rooted sectarian feeling in the Riverstown district. As we have seen, many of the Protestant witnesses at the conspiracy trial appeared to be on friendly terms with some of the defendants and the authorities reported that the few Protestants who actually submitted

5 John Stenson memorial at Riverstown

and subscribed to the league were not interfered with. The possibility that some of the Protestant witnesses exaggerated the extent of their friendship with the defendants, in order to defuse any further persecution, certainly has to be considered. It might also be argued that the rank and file members of Riverstown UIL were simply carrying out the orders of the branch leaders but whether or not this was done in a voluntary capacity or through fear is another question. It may well have been that the leaders of the campaign were concerned with trade in Riverstown and were attempting to benefit at the expense of rival Protestant businesses by forcing their fellow Catholics to boycott such premises. The Irish authorities believed that 'the prime movers in all this boycotting were shopkeepers, who, however, took care to consider their own interests and did not refuse to supply goods to any one'.[14] Indeed, evidence in court revealed that the president of Rivertown UIL, Thomas J. Judge, was still profiting financially from Protestant customers despite the boycott that was meant to be in place against them. There may also have been resentment that Protestants had benefited as much as Catholics from the Wyndham Land Act of 1903, which the UIL believed was a product of their agitation.[15]

Although there were claims by the *Roscommon Herald* and by the secretary of Riverstown UIL, Thomas Cawley, that the police had fired without provocation at the crowd on the night Stenson was shot, the evidence would appear to suggest otherwise. Prior to the tragedy there were numerous incidents and reports of firearms being used in the Riverstown area in the presence of the police. Even the principal nationalist newspaper, the *Freeman's Journal*, reported that shots had been fired from the crowd on the night. The actions of the police were strongly defended by the RIC County Inspector and by the Liberal government who held that they had acted with restraint and were under the control of their commanding officer. However, the limited nature of the inquest and the absence of a full public inquiry left a question mark over the shooting, leaving the Liberal government open to accusations that they were anxious to hush up the whole affair. While the chief secretary, Augustine Birrell, did send someone down to Riverstown to privately enquire into the incident, his refusal to grant an inquiry played into the hands of those who wished to perpetuate the idea of a government cover up.

While the shooting of John Stenson was a local incident, it had an effect on the national debate on law and order which was raging at the time. While the government was anxious to rule by the ordinary law the Conservatives and unionists were keen to see the implementation of the Crimes Act, which they believed was the only answer to the cattle-driving agitation which had characterized the Ranch War. Irish unionists such as Sir Edward Carson, John Lonsdale and the marquess of Lansdowne seized on the Stenson incident and the actions of the Riverstown UIL towards Protestants to pressurize the Liberal government on the issue of law and order. The inability of the police to effectively combat the agitation at Riverstown and the actions of the predominantly nationalist magisterial bench at Riverstown courthouse who refused to send the defendants forward for trial, further convinced unionists that the ordinary law had failed in many western districts. The frequency with which firearms were used in the region, culminating in the exchange of fire on the night Stenson was shot, highlighted the consequences of allowing the

Peace Preservation (Ireland) Act, 1881 to lapse. Shortly before the Stenson incident the chief secretary, Augustine Birrell, had admitted in the house of commons that there had 'been a considerable increase in the number of offences in which firearms have been used' in the two years since the act had not been in force.[16]

In death, Stenson joined the gallery of Irish patriots who had sacrificed their lives in the fight against England. A popular mythology, propagated to a large degree by the *Sligo Champion*, quickly developed around Stenson; he was the subject of numerous poems which appeared in that newspaper (see Appendix D). Mary Delia Gilmartin's poem compared John Stenson to Protestant patriots such as Robert Emmet and Lord Edward FitzGerald who had also lost their lives fighting for Ireland; this was somewhat ironic given the UIL campaign against Protestants in Riverstown.[17] Patrick Higgins' poem, 'The Stenson murder', portrayed Stenson as a martyr and compared him to the men who had fought in the 1798 rebellion. In Higgins' version of events, Stenson was murdered, by the 'bloodhounds' of Dublin Castle, 'on behalf of Erin's cause' while fighting 'oppressive laws'.[18] Stenson was also the subject of an anti-enlistment poster circulated in Enniscorthy, Co. Wexford, at the beginning of 1909, which condemned recruitment to the British army and to the RIC. The poster called on Irish men not to become 'one of the creatures in England's pay who evicted your fathers, and would do the same with their own; one of the men who shot young Stenson and would shoot you tomorrow'.[19]

Inspired by the laying of the Stenson memorial foundation stone on 31 October 1909 Michael Daly, a member of Geevagh UIL, recited a poem at a branch meeting shortly after. That poem demonstrated how the incident at Riverstown had become much more than a simple cattle-drive, but was now remembered as the day that the men of Riverstown 'withstood the forces of the crown' in battle, until the death of the 'martyred hero, Stenson'.[20] Little remains today in the modern village of Riverstown to remind the visitor of the events that occurred there over one hundred years ago, however; almost hidden away at the back of the village overlooking wide open fields is the statue of John Stenson. Immortalized in stone as a ranch warrior, he is a poignant reminder of the days when his name and that of Riverstown reverberated throughout Ireland and Westminster and as far afield as the United States of America.

APPENDIX A. PRINCIPAL MEMBERS OF RIVERSTOWN UIL BRANCH: MAY 1908–JUNE 1909

Surname	First name	Position	Townland	DED	Age in 1911	Marital status	Occupation	Religion	Miscellaneous
Judge	Thomas J.	President	Riverstown	Riverstown	27*	Single	Shopkeeper	Catholic	Not in Sligo in the 1911 census. He is in Ballintogher town in 1901 aged 27.
O'Gara	Thomas	Vice-president	Riverstown	Riverstown	45	Married	Builder	Catholic	
Moran	Patrick	Treasurer	Ardkeeran	Riverstown	51	Married	Farmer	Catholic	His father Denis is a 'farmer'
Cawley	Thomas	Secretary	Emlagh	Riverstown	45	Unmarried	Farm servant	Catholic	Living and working for his relatives who are also Cawleys
McGoldrick	Peter	Secretary	Ogham	Riverstown	48	Single	Farmer	Catholic	His father James is a 'farmer'
McDermott	John	Deputy vice-president	Riverstown	Riverstown				Catholic	The son of Bernard McDermott. John is not living at home in 1911.
McDermott	James	Committee member	Riverstown	Riverstown	62	Married	Shopkeeper	Catholic	
Deignan	Patrick	Committee member	Ardkeeran	Riverstown	46	Married	Engine driver in creamery	Catholic	
Culhane	Thomas F.	Committee member	Riverstown	Riverstown	41	Married	Shopkeeper & farmer	Catholic	
Ellis	Martin	Committee member	Ardcumber	Riverstown	33	Married	General Labourer	Catholic	
Anderson	William	Committee member	Emlagh	Riverstown	38	Unmarried	Farmer	Catholic	His father James is a 'farmer'
Tighe	James	Committee member	Rosmore	Riverstown	33	Unmarried	Farmer's son	Catholic	His father John is a 'farmer'
McDonagh	Martin	Committee member	Rusheen	Ballynakill	31	Unmarried	Farmer	Catholic	His father Patrick is a 'farmer'
Cawley	Charles	Committee member	Emlagh	Riverstown	39	Married	Farmer	Catholic	Relative of the secretary, Thomas Cawley, who works for him as a 'farm servant'
Taheny	Michael	Committee member	Emlagh	Riverstown	53	Married	Farmer	Catholic	
Candon	Mark	Committee member	Carrowkeel	Riverstown	52	Married	Farmer	Catholic	His father William is still alive
Beirne	Thomas	Committee member	Cultidangan	Drumcolumb	43	Married	Farmer	Catholic	
Carvey	James	Committee member	Tawnagh	Lakeview	24*	Single	Agricultural labourer	Catholic	Given as Jame Carvey aged 24 in 1901

Surname	First name	Position	Townland	DED	Age in 1911	Marital status	Occupation	Religion	Miscellaneous
Jinks	John	Committee member	Ardneeskan	Lisconny	40	Single	Farmer's son	Catholic	His father William is still alive
Byrne	Martin	Committee member	Drumdoney	Killadoon	55	Married	Farmer	Catholic	
Sweeney	Patrick	Committee member	Whitehill	Lakeview	33	Single	Tailor	Catholic	His father Patrick Sweeney, a 'farmer', is 69 in 1911 census. Could be him and not the son.
Leonard	Joe	Committee member	Tawnagh	Lakeview	34	Single	Car and cart builder	Catholic	
Nangle	James	Committee member	Drumraine	Lakeview	42	Married	Farmer	Catholic	
Flannery	Bryan	Committee member	Ardneeskan	Riverstown	46	Single	Farmer's son	Catholic	His mother Mary listed as a 'farmer'
Callaghan	John	Committee member	Lisconny	Lisconny	75	Married	Farmer	Catholic	
Healey	Pat	Committee member	Rusheen	Ballynakill	57	Single	Farmer	Catholic	
McDonagh	Edward	Committee member	Carrownspurraun	Lisconny	36	Single	Farmer's son	Catholic	His father Luke is as 'farmer'
O'Hara	Charles	Committee member	Lisconny	Lisconny	69	Married	Farmer	Catholic	
Scanlon	J.	Committee member	Carrownagark	Drumfin		Married	Farmer	Catholic	There is a James (35) and a John (53) Scanlon in Carrownagark. It could be either man.
Mulligan	Tim	Committee member	Lisbanagher	Lisconny	32	Single	Farmer	Catholic	No one by this name here in 1901 or 1911 census
Kesney	P.	Committee member	Carrowreagh						
Lyons	James	Committee member	Knockanarrow	Lisconny	40	Married	Farmer	Catholic	
Sheerin	James	Committee member	Carrowcashel	Riverstown	36	Single	Victualler	Catholic	No record of him in 1901 or 1911
Beirne	Pat	Committee member							
Kerins	James	Committee member	Ogham	Riverstown	46	Single	Farmer	Catholic	Father still alive
Lavin	J.	Committee member	Drumcolumb	Drumcolumb				Catholic	There are two men named James Lavin in Drumcolumb. One is a married 'farmer' aged 60, the other an unmarried 'farm servant' aged 28.

★ age in 1901 census.
Source: Census of Ireland, 1901; Census of Ireland, 1911; *Sligo Champion*, 6 June 1908.

APPENDIX B. DEFENDANTS IN THE RIVERSTOWN CONSPIRACY CASE

Surname	First name	Townland	DED	Age in 1911	Marital status	Occupation	Religion	Miscellanous
Devaney	John	Carrowcashel	Riverstown	79	Married	Labourer	Catholic	Carried Thomas Higgin's milk
Ellis	Martin	Ardcumber	Riverstown	33	Married	General labourer	Catholic	
Flannery	Bryan	Ardneeskan	Riverstown	46	Single	Farmer's son	Catholic	His mother Mary listed as a 'farmer'
Higgins	Bernard	Drumfin	Drumfin	67	Married	Farmer	Catholic	Carried milk for James Johnston junior and Jane Allen
Kearns	James	Ogham	Riverstown	46	Single	Farmer	Catholic	He is James Kerins in the 1911 census.
King	William J.	Drumfin	Drumfin	35	Single	Blacksmith	Catholic	His mother Bridget King is a 'farmer'
McDermott	Bernard	Riverstown	Riverstown	65	Married	Blacksmith & farmer	Catholic	His son is called John McDermott
McDermott	John	Riverstown	Riverstown				Catholic	Son of Bernard McDermott
McDonagh	Edward (Luke)	Carrownspurraun	Lisconny	36	Single	Farmer's son	Catholic	His father Luke is still alive in the 1911 census
McDonagh	Pat	Carrownspurraun	Lisconny	62	Married	Farmer	Catholic	Carried Thomas Middleton's milk
Morrison	Mathew	Drumfin	Drumfin	35	Single	Farmer	Catholic	His father James is a 'farmer'
O'Gara	Thomas	Riverstown	Riverstown	45	Married	Builder	Catholic	
O'Hara	Charles	Lisconny	Lisconny	69	Married	Farmer	Catholic	
Sheerin	James	Carrowcashel	Riverstown	36	Single	Victualler	Catholic	
Sweeney	Patrick	Whitehill	Lakeview	33	Single	Tailor	Catholic	His father Patrick Sweeney, a 'farmer', is 69 in 1911 census.
Tonry	William	Drumfin	Drumfin	50	Married	Farmer	Catholic	He is William Tonra in the 1901 census. Carried milk for James Johnston senior, William Clifford and Charles O'Connor
Tonry	Michael	Drumfin	Drumfin	62	Married	Farmer	Catholic	

Source: 'Crown Solicitors Office. Riverstown conspiracy case' (National Archives of Ireland, Chief Secretary's Office Registered Papers (CSORP), 1909, 8820); Census of Ireland, 1901; Census of Ireland, 1911.

APPENDIX C. PROTESTANT WITNESSES IN THE RIVERSTOWN CONSPIRACY CASE

Surname	First name	Townland	DED	Occupation	Age in 1911	Marital status	Miscellanous
Allen	Jane	Murrilyroe	Riverstown	Farmer	70	Widower	
Bright	Henry	Carrownspurraun	Lisconny	Farmer	48	Married	
Bright	James	Turnalaydan	Lisconny	Farmer	46	Widower	
Clifford	William	Carrowkeel	Riverstown	Farmer	29	Single	
Harte	Edward	Whitehill	Lakeview	Farmer	64	Married	
Harte	Thomas	Whitehill	Lakeview				Thomas and John Harte are brothers. Thomas does not appear in 1901 or 1911. Spelt Hartte in 1911 census
Harte	John	Whitehill	Lakeview	Farmer	44	Single	
Higgins	Thomas	Ardcumber	Riverstown	Farmer	66	Married	
Johnston	James (senior)	Drumfin	Drumfin	Farmer	69	Married	
Johnston	James (junior)	Drumfin	Drumfin	Farmer	57	Married	There appears to be a difficulty with the ages given by James Johnston senior and junior
Meredith	Elizabeth	Tobernaglashy	Riverstown	Farmer	53	Widower	
Middleton	George	Carrownspurraun	Lisconny	Retired farmer	74	Widower	
Morrison	Thomas	Drumfin	Drumfin	Farmer	48	Single	
O'Connor	Charles						
Rowlette	Margaret	Behy	Riverstown	Farmer	62	Single	

Source: *Sligo Independent*, 7 Nov. 1907; Census of Ireland, 1901; Census of Ireland, 1911.

APPENDIX D. POEMS ABOUT JOHN STENSON PUBLISHED IN THE *SLIGO CHAMPION*

Mary Delia Martin, '*Lines written for "Sligo Champion" in memory of the late John Stinson [sic], at the request of _____, Co. Sligo*'

Dear Ireland, thy patriots yet
Are countless I can see,
Though many a good man died in vain
For love, asthore, of thee.

Ah! died in vain, I should not say,
Since hopeful still thou art
To fold thy sons and daughters free
To thy maternal heart

And he who fell in freedom's fight,
Aged or in life's bloom,
One link at least in slavery's chain
Went with him to the tomb.

And who was he met with his death
In freedom's fight just now,
Before the sun of twenty summers
Shone on his boyish brow.

It was the noble hearted John
Round whom such promise hung,
That proudly stood for right, 'tis said,
Too daring and too young.

As brave a youth that ever stepped
 Upon the shamrocked sod,
Whose name in record shall be kept
In climes he never trod.

Emmet parted with his love,
Fitzgerald with his wife,
For the sake of their dear native land
In the very prime of life.

Now, Stenson passing his tender teens,
Was snapped from his sister one.
Who'll say it 'twas not because he thought
To finish what they begun?

No more, as only a brother could,
Fond word to her he'll speak
With the merry twinkle in his eye
And the fresh rose on his cheek.

Ah! you, ye lovers of Ireland,
At home and far away,
Should think of this poor orphan boy
Whene'er you kneel to pray.

Remember young John Stinson's fate,
Had heaven decreed it so,
He fell in freedom's fight as well
As those of long ago.

5 Dec. 1908

Patrick Higgins, 'The Stenson murder'

On the 29th day of October, nineteen hundred and eight,
On a grazing ranch at Riverstown John Stenson meet his fate.
He little dreamt his days were spent when he entered the field,
Until his comrades and himself were quickly forced to yield.

But the bloodhounds were so thirsty, their bullets showed no lack,
They did not value human life to spare the bullock's back,
The murderer that shot him he surely took his aim,
Poor Stenson stood in range of him and was shot right through the brain.

But the cowards showed no mercy, and well they know he fell,
The bullets showered around him, like bluring shot and shell,
But their orders were "to fire, and shot them if you can,
We have the Castle at our back, so don't spare any man."

The cruel law of England may try to quash it down
By bring other claims against the men of Riverstown;
But we'll make the English Saxons in all their cunning strife
To try the wilful murderer who took John Stenson's life.

That voice is stilled for ever that his country loved to hear,
That manly form is vanished that thrilled with hope and cheer;
But he was a brave young fellow, he'll be number with the great,
For he truly died a martyr, like the men of ninety-eight.

On the green fields of Ardcumber, on behalf of Erin's cause,
Twas in that strife he lost his life, against oppressive laws;
But Ireland shall ne'er forget the noble work he done.

With hand and heart he led the band and stood before the gun.

He's dead, the noble and the brave, but his spirit still lives on,
Among the men of Riverstown, in history and in song,
It's with his dearest brother and loving sisters two
We sympathise sincerely in bidding them adieu.

In loving memory to his name these lines I do pen down,
He was a credit to his name in dear old Riverstown;
And we do pray that from this day your hazels will be staunch,
And do not spare the bullocks hair when you catch them on the ranch.

And let true men, like you, men, be good enough to share,
And offer up to heaven a fervent little prayer
That God in all His mercy has chosen for the best,
To take poor John to heaven to mingle with the best.

2 Jan. 1909

Poem by Michael Daly

This morning early I arose,
As the sun in the east was appearing,
From out the hills rode a warrior bold,
And green was the coat he was wearing.
He addressed me then in his Irish tone,
And told me what was his intention –
He said he was going to see the spot
Where fell the brave John Stenson.

Then I went with him to Riverstown,
We were filled with admiration,
The green and gold did promptly wave
In a grand demonstration.
I saw a mass of sturdy men
And colleens bright and winsome
Upon the sod that was enriched
With the blood of poor John Stenson.

Brave Charlie Cogan then arose,
And addressed the meeting loudly:
He said "Boys look on yonder spot
And gaze upon it proudly;
Twas there a noble fight was waged
By heroes bold unflinching.

Until it ended with the death
Of our martyred hero, Stenson.

Twas there the men of Riverstown,
On the spot where you now are gazing,
Withstood the forces of the crown
With rifle fire blazing.
Though unprepared they fought their way
And their wounds with gore were drenching,
Till deadlier still, a bullet flew
And killed the gallant Stenson."

Then many a veteran bosom rose
While many a band was marching –
Scanlon, O'Dowd, and Sheehy were there,
Bernard Conlon, and John Gilmartin,
And many a noble face I saw,
Whose names are beyond all mention;
The Connaught clans were marshaled there
To honour young John Stenson.

And grand was the sight for to behold
On Ardcumber ranch that evening,
For many's the banner of green and gold
In the sunset rays were streaming.
There were numerous contingents there,
Their names would be hard to mention,
And many a voice did curse the men
That murdered poor John Stenson.

To raise a noble monument,
It was their resolution,
To remember him when our country would
For Irish men will rule this land,
When they banish the landlords' henchmen
And honour her heroes proud and grand –
For such was bold John Stenson.

13 Nov. 1909

Notes

ABBREVIATIONS

CI Sligo	National Archives of Ireland, RIC County Inspector's monthly report for Sligo
CO	Colonial Office
COI 1901	Census of Ireland, 1901, Household Returns for Co. Sligo available at: http://www.census.nationalarchives.ie/
COI 1911	Census of Ireland, 1911, Household Returns for Co. Sligo available at: http://www.census.nationalarchives.ie/
CSORP	National Archives of Ireland, Chief Secretary's Office Registered Papers
DL	Deputy Lieutenant
FJ	*Freeman's Journal*
Hansard 4	*The parliamentary debates*, fourth series, 1892–1908 (vols i–cxcix, London, 1892–1909)
Hansard 5	*The parliamentary debates*, fifth series, *House of Commons*, 1909–42 (vols i–cccxciii, London, 1909–42)
HC	House of Commons
IG	RIC Inspector General
IT	*Irish Times*
NAI	National Archives of Ireland, Dublin
RH	*Roscommon Herald*
SC	*Sligo Champion*
SI	*Sligo Independent*
TNA	The National Archives (UK), London

INTRODUCTION

1 *Hansard 4*, cxcvi, 1826 (23 Nov. 1908).

2 Paul Bew, *Conflict and conciliation in Ireland, 1890–1910: Parnellites and radical agrarians* (Oxford, 1987), p. 140 and Fergus Campbell, *Land and revolution: nationalist politics in the west of Ireland 1891–1921* (Oxford, 2005), p. 102.

3 See Laurence Geary, *The Plan of Campaign, 1886–91* (Cork, 1986). The Plan of Campaign was a scheme, promoted by leading nationalists such as Timothy Healy, William O'Brien and John Dillon to compel the reduction of rents on certain estates by the collective action of their tenants. See S.J. Connolly, (ed.), *Oxford companion to Irish history* (2nd ed., Oxford, 2004), p. 468.

4 James McGuire and James Quinn (eds), *Dictionary of Irish biography*, 9 vols (Cambridge, 2009), vi, pp 13–14. See also Íde Ní Liatháin, *The life and career of P.A. McHugh: a north Connacht politician, 1859–1909* (Dublin, 1999).

5 Michael Farry, *Sligo 1914–1921: a chronicle of conflict* (Meath, 1992), p. 2 and Fergus Campbell, *The Irish establishment, 1879–1914* (Oxford, 2009), p. 167. The Irish National Land League was established in 1879 and was the principal tenant organisation during the period of agrarian agitation from 1879 to 1881, known as the Land War.

6 *SC*, 5 Sept. 1908.

7 Jack Johnston (ed.), *The Riverstown story, County Sligo* (Riverstown, 2005), p. 11.

8 *Census of Ireland, 1901. Part I. Area, houses, and population: also the ages, civil or*

conjugal condition, occupations, birthplaces,
religion, and education of the people. Vol. iv.
Province of Connaught. No. 5 County of
Sligo, 69–98 [Cd. 1059] HC 1902,
cxxviii.

9 *Report of the estates commissioners for the
year ending 31 March 1909 and for the
period from 1st November 1903 to 31st
March 1909*, 80–81, [Cd.4849] HC 1909,
xxiii, 737.

10 *Return of untenanted lands in rural
districts, distinguishing demesnes on which
there is a mansion, showing: rural district
and electoral division; townland; area in
statute acres; valuation (poor law); names of
occupiers as in valuation lists*, 389–97,
C.177, HC 1906, 250. The figures for
Lisconny and Ballynakill include a
mansion house/demesne.

11 *Report of the royal commission on
congestion in Ireland. Sixth report*, 289,
[Cd.3748] HC 1908, xxxix, 701.

12 *Report of the royal commission on
congestion in Ireland. Sixth report*, 93,
[Cd.3748] HC 1908, xxxix, 701.

13 David Seth Jones, *Graziers, land reform and
political conflict in Ireland* (Washington,
1995); Miriam Moffitt, *The Church of
Ireland community of Killala and Achonry,
1870–1940: thinly scattered* (Dublin, 1999),
and, idem, 'Protestant tenant farmers and
the land league in north Connacht' in
Carla King and Conor McNamara (eds),
*The west of Ireland: new perspectives on the
nineteenth century* (Dublin, 2011), pp 93–
116. Paul Bew, *Conflict and conciliation in
Ireland, 1890–1910: Parnellites and radical
agrarians* (Oxford, 1987); Philip Bull,
*Land, politics and nationalism: a study of the
Irish land question* (Dublin, 1996); Fergus
Campbell, *Land and revolution: nationalist
politics in the west of Ireland, 1891–1921*
(Oxford, 2005).

1. 'THE LAW OF THE LEAGUE'

1 *Hansard 4*, cxciii, 1803 (30 July 1908).
2 *IT*, 9 Mar. 1908.
3 CI Sligo, Aug. 1908.
4 CI Sligo, Mar. 1908.
5 S.J. Connolly, *The Oxford companion to
Irish history* (Oxford, 2nd edition 2004),
p. 509.

6 CI Sligo, Apr. 1908.
7 CI Sligo, Apr. 1908. For more on UIL
justice see Campbell, *Land and
revolution*, pp 124–65.
8 CI Sligo, Feb. 1909.
9 CI Sligo, Apr. 1908.
10 CI Sligo, Feb. 1909.
11 CI Sligo, Apr. 1908. In this context 'car'
refers to a horse and carriage or a horse
and cart rather than a motorised
vehicle.
12 *SC*, 11 Apr. 1908.
13 *Essex County Standard*, 11 Apr. 1908,
cited in *SC*, 25 Apr. 1908.
14 *SC*, 2 May 1908.
15 *SC*, 16 May 1908.
16 *SC*, 16 May 1908; CI Sligo, May 1908.
17 Led by Sir Leander Starr Jameson in
1895, the Jameson raid was a failed
attempt to claim the Boer Transvaal
Republic for the British Empire.
18 CI Sligo, Oct. 1908.
19 COI 1901; Jack Johnston (ed.), *The
Riverstown story, County Sligo*
(Riverstown, 2005), pp 51–4.
20 COI 1911.
21 *SC*, 6 June 1908.
22 CI Sligo, Oct. 1908.
23 *SC*, 13 and 27 June 1908.
24 *SC*, 27 June 1908.
25 *SC*, 2 May 1908.
26 See *Hansard 4*, cxciv, 609–10 (16 Oct.
1908) and *IT*, 28 Aug. 1907.
27 *Hansard 4*, cxciv, 609–10 (16 Oct. 1908);
CI Sligo, June 1908.
28 *SC*, 4 July 1908.
29 CI Sligo, June 1908.
30 *SC*, 18 July 1908.
31 CI Sligo, Jun. 1908.
32 CI Sligo July 1908.
33 *SC*, 18 July 1908.
34 CI Sligo, June 1908.
35 CI Sligo, July 1908.
36 CI Sligo, July and Aug. 1908.
37 CI Sligo, Aug. 1908.
38 *RH*, 5 Sept. 1908.
39 Regardless of their denomination,
people not of the Roman Catholic
Church who were approached to join
or subscribe to the UIL were usually
termed as 'Protestants' in contemporary
sources; for clarity and continuity, this
term has also been applied here.
40 *SI*, 22 Aug. 1908.

41 *IT*, 10 Sept. 1908.
42 CI Sligo, Sept. 1908; *SI*, 14 Nov. 1908.
43 *SC*, 12 Sept. 1908.
44 CI Sligo, Aug. 1908.
45 *SI*, 22 Aug. 1908.
46 CI Sligo, Aug. 1908.
47 CI Sligo, Sept. 1908; *SI*, 14 Nov. 1908.
48 *SC*, 26 Sept. 1908.
49 CI Sligo, Sept. 1908; 'County Sligo.
     Ballymote district. Riverstown
     conspiracy case' (TNA, CO 904/121).
50 *SC*, 3 Oct. 1908.

2. THE SHOOTING OF JOHN STENSON
        AND ITS AFTERMATH

 1 CI Sligo, Oct. 1908.
 2 CI Sligo, Oct. 1908; *RH*, 14 and 28
     Nov. 1908.
 3 *SC*, 24 Oct. 1908.
 4 *SC*, 31 Oct. 1908; *RH*, 31 Oct. 1908; CI
     Sligo, Oct. 1908.
 5 *SI*, 31 Oct. 1908 and *FJ*, 30 Oct. 1908.
 6 *IT*, 30 Oct. 1908; *FJ*, 30 Oct. 1908.
 7 *IT*, 30 Oct. 1908.
 8 Ibid.
 9 CI Sligo, Oct. 1908.
10 *Hansard 4*, cxcvi, 1414–18 (19 Nov.
     1908) and 'County Sligo. Ballymote
     district. Death of John Stenson. Attack
     on the police at Riverstown' (TNA,
     CO 904/121).
11 CI Sligo, Oct. 1908.
12 *SI*, 31 Oct. 1908.
13 *RH*, 7 Nov. 1908.
14 See *RH*, 7 and 14 Nov. 1908.
15 *Hansard 4*, cxcv, 1409–11 (5 Nov. 1908).
16 S.J. Connolly (ed.), *Oxford companion to
     Irish history* (2nd ed., Oxford, 2004), p.
     108; *Weekly Irish Times*, 10 Feb. 1906.
17 *Hansard 4*, cxcv, 1409–11 (5 Nov. 1908).
18 *SI*, 3 Oct. 1908.
19 *Times*, 31 Oct. 1908.
20 *Irish Catholic*, 7 Nov. 1908.
21 *Irish Independent*, 12 Dec. 1906.
22 I.G. monthly report for Nov. 1908.
23 *RH*, 7 Nov. 1908.
24 COI 1911; 'The Crown Solicitors
     Office. Riverstown conspiracy case'
     (NAI, CSORP 1909, 8820).
25 *SC*, 6 Feb. 1909.

26 CI Sligo, Dec. 1908.
27 CI Sligo, Oct. 1908.
28 CI Sligo, Dec. 1908.
29 CI Sligo, Dec. 1908.
30 *SC*, 5 Dec. 1908.
31 *IT*, 6 Nov. 1908.
32 *Irish Facts*, Dec. 1908.
33 *IT*, 14 May 1909.
34 *RH*, 7 Nov. 1908.
35 *RH*, 7 Nov. 1908; 'County Sligo.
     Ballymote district. Riverstown
     conspiracy case' (TNA, CO 904/121).
36 *RH*, 7 Nov. 1908 and *SI*, 7 Nov. 1908.
37 *Hansard 4*, cxcvii, 684–6 (26 Nov. 1908).
38 *Hansard 5 (Commons)*, iv, 333 (28 Apr.
     1909).
39 *IT*, 7 Nov. 1908.
40 *IT*, 16 Nov. 1908.
41 *The Times* (London), 11 Nov. 1908;
     'County Sligo. Ballymote district.
     Riverstown conspiracy case' (TNA,
     CO 904/121).
42 *IT*, 9 Nov. 1908.
43 *SI*, 28 Nov. 1908.
44 *IT*, 13 Nov. 1908.

3. THE 'RIVERSTOWN CONSPIRACY'
               CASE

 1 CI Sligo, Nov. 1908.
 2 *RH*, 14 Nov. 1908.
 3 'County Sligo. Ballymote district.
     Riverstown conspiracy case' (TNA,
     CO 904/121).
 4 *Hansard 4*, cxcvi, 1231–32 (18 Nov. 1908).
 5 *Sinn Féin*, 7 Nov. 1908, quoted in *Irish
     Facts*, Dec. 1908, p. 492.
 6 *Hansard 4*, cxcvi, 1414–18 (19 Nov. 1908).
 7 *Weekly Irish Times*, 16 Jan. 1909.
 8 *Times* (London), 21 Nov. 1908.
 9 *SI*, 14 Nov. 1908.
10 CI Sligo, Jan. 1909.
11 *SC*, 6 Feb. 1909.
12 *SC*, 6 Feb. 1909.
13 *SC*, 6 Feb. 1909.
14 CI Sligo, Aug. 1908.
15 *SC*, 6 Feb. 1909.
16 See *IT*, 5 Feb. 1909 and *SC*, 6 Feb. 1909.
17 See *SC*, 5 Sept. 1908 and *Hansard 5
     (Commons)*, iv, 724 (3 May 1909).
18 COI 1911.
19 *IT*, 13 Feb. 1909.

20 *Hansard 5 (Commons)*, i, 741–55 (24 Feb. 1909).
21 CI Sligo, Feb. 1909.
22 *SC*, 27 Feb. 1909.
23 *IT,* 11 Mar. 1909.
24 CI Sligo, Mar. 1909.
25 *IT*, 1 May 1909.
26 *SC*, 19 Sept. 1908. See *IT*, 14 May 1909.
27 *IT*, 14 May 1909.
28 *IT*, 15 May 1909.
29 *IT*, 15 May 1909.
30 *Hansard 5 (Commons)*, xiv, 848 (2 Mar. 1910).
31 CI Sligo, Dec. 1908.
32 *SC*, 30 Jan. 1909.
33 CI Sligo, Feb. 1909
34 *SC*, 20 Feb. 1909.
35 Alvin Jackson, *Ireland 1798–1998* (Oxford, 1999), p. 159. See also Paul Bew, *Conflict and conciliation: Parnellities and radical agrarians* (Oxford, 1987), pp 204–7.
36 *SC*, 20 Feb. 1909.
37 *SC*, 20 Feb. 1909.
38 *SC*, 2 Jan. and 13 Mar. 1909.
39 CI Sligo, Dec. 1908.
40 *SC*, 6 Mar. 1909.
41 CI Sligo, Feb. 1909
42 CI Sligo, Apr. 1909.
43 *Hansard 5 (Commons)*, iv, 1976 (12 May 1910).
44 *SC*, 22 May 1909.
45 See *RH,* 29 May 1909 and CI Sligo, May 1909.
46 *SC*, 21 Aug. 1909.
47 CI Sligo, July 1909
48 CI Sligo, Nov. 1909.

CONCLUSION

1 *SC*, 4 Sept. 1909.
2 *SI*, 4 Sept. 1909.
3 *SC*, 30 Oct. 1909.
4 *SC*, 6 Nov. 1909.
5 *SC*, 6 Nov. 1909; *IT*, 8 Nov. 1908.
6 *SC*, 20 Nov. 1909.
7 *SC*, 24 July, 30 Oct. 1908 and 21 May 1910.
8 *SC*, 23 July 1910.
9 *SC*, 17 July 1909.
10 *Connacht Tribune*, 30 July 1910; *FJ*, 23 July 1910.
11 *FJ*, 16 Aug. 1910.
12 See *FJ,* 16 Aug. 1910, and *SC*, 20 Aug. 1910.
13 *Irish Independent*, 29 Aug. 1910.
14 'County Sligo. Ballymote district. Riverstown conspiracy case' (TNA, CO 904/121).
15 *IT*, 14 May 1909.
16 *Hansard 4*, cxciv, 716 (19 Oct. 1908).
17 *SC*, 5 Dec. 1908.
18 Patrick Higgins, 'The Stenson Murder' in *SC*, 2 Jan. 1909.
19 *Irish Facts*, Feb. 1909, p. 109.
20 *SC*, 13 Nov. 1909.